Acrobat® 7.0

Level 2

Harleen Kaur Sethi
Aarthi Janet Gunaseelan

Acrobat® 7.0: Level 2

Part Number: 084173
Course Edition: 1.0

Acknowledgments

Project Team

Content Developer: Harleen Kaur Sethi and Aarthi Janet Gunaseelan • **Content Manager:** Chris Clark and Christopher Worden • **Graphic Designer:** Vasanth K • **Project Coordinator:** AnilKumar Singh • **Media Instructional Designer:** Harleen Kaur Sethi and Aarthi Janet Gunaseelan • **Content Editor:** Sindhu Sreekumar • **Materials Editor:** Gayathri L and Anbuselvan A • **Business Matter Expert:** • **Technical Reviewer:** • **Project Technical Support:** Mike Toscano

NOTICES

Adobe Certified Expert (ACE) Program:

The Adobe Certified Expert (ACE) Program logo that appears on the cover indicates that this courseware addresses ACE exam objectives.

Acrobat® 7.0: Level 2

Lesson 1: Creating PDFs from Technical Documents

Lesson 2: Enhancing PDF Documents

Contents

ABOUT THIS COURSE

As a workplace professional with some experience in using Adobe Acrobat, you are now ready to further develop your PDF documents. In this course, you will use Adobe Acrobat® 7.0 Professional to convert technical documents to PDF files, enhance and control PDF content accessibility, customize PDF documents for interactive use online, and prepare PDFs for commercial printing.

Whether you are creating PDFs for a commercial printer to print, for people to view on different display platforms, such as a PDA, or for people with different visibility requirements, Acrobat enables you to accommodate those diverse needs by ensuring that everyone in your audience will be able to access and view the document the way you intended it to appear.

Course Description

Target Student

The audience may or may not be creative and/or print professionals.

Course Prerequisites

Acrobat® 7.0: Level 1

How to Use This Book

As a Learning Guide

Each lesson covers one broad topic or set of related topics. Lessons are arranged in order of increasing proficiency with *Acrobat Professional*; skills you acquire in one lesson are used and developed in subsequent lessons. For this reason, you should work through the lessons in sequence.

We organized each lesson into results-oriented topics. Topics include all the relevant and supporting information you need to master *Acrobat Professional*, and activities allow you to apply this information to practical hands-on examples.

You get to try out each new skill on a specially prepared sample file. This saves you typing time and allows you to concentrate on the skill at hand. Through the use of sample files, hands-on activities, illustrations that give you feedback at crucial steps, and supporting background information, this book provides you with the foundation and structure to learn *Acrobat Professional* quickly and easily.

As a Review Tool

Any method of instruction is only as effective as the time and effort you are willing to invest in it. In addition, some of the information that you learn in class may not be important to you immediately, but it may become important later on. For this reason, we encourage you to spend some time reviewing the topics and activities after the course. For additional challenge when reviewing activities, try the "What You Do" column before looking at the "How You Do It" column.

As a Reference

The organization and layout of the book make it easy to use as a learning tool and as an after-class reference. You can use this book as a first source for definitions of terms, background information on given topics, and summaries of procedures.

Course Objectives

In this course, you will use Adobe Acrobat® 7.0 Professional to convert technical documents to PDF files, enhance and control PDF content accessibility, customize PDF documents for interactive use online, and prepare PDFs for commercial printing.

You will:

- create PDFs from technical documents.
- enhance the utility and accessibility of PDF documents.
- create interactive PDF forms.
- begin preparing a PDF document for commercial printing.
- create composite and color separation prints from a PDF document.

Course Requirements

Hardware

- An Intel® Pentium® processor.
- 128 MB of RAM (256 MB or greater is recommended).
- A minimum of 555 MB of available hard-disk space.
- A CD-ROM drive if installing from a CD.
- A mouse or compatible tracking device.
- A 1024 x 768 screen resolution.
- A projection system to display the instructor's computer screen.

Software

- Adobe® Acrobat 7 Professional for Windows.
- Microsoft® Internet Explorer 5.01 or later.
- Microsoft® Office Visio 2003 is preferable, but not mandatory, to complete one activity.
- Adobe® Photoshop 7.0.1.
- Microsoft® Excel.
- Windows Media Player

Class Setup

1. In order to ensure that all features of Acrobat Professional 6 will be available for this course, run a standard installation from the software installation CD-ROM.
2. You will also need to run additional software as described in the Course Requirements section. Perform a standard or full installation of the applications you use in addition to Acrobat Professional.
3. This course will run best if Acrobat's preferences are set to their default values. To reset settings, you could uninstall Acrobat, then reinstall using the Adobe Acrobat installation CD-ROM.
4. On the course CD-ROM, open the 084_173 folder. Then, open the Data folder. Run the 084173dd.exe self-extracting file located within. This will install a folder named 084173Data on your C drive. Move the contents of the 084173Data folder to the following location: C:\Documents and Settings\Administrator\My Documents\. This folder contains all the data files that you will use to complete this course.
5. This course specifies the use of certain fonts. If these fonts are not installed, the documents the student works on will not display as intended. Make sure the fonts Arial and Freestyle Script are installed on the computer.
6. This course will run most smoothly if your monitor resolution is set to at least 1024 x 768 pixels-per-inch.
7. You need to install two PostScript Printer Description files and add two printers for the Printing lesson. The course data includes URL bookmark files that you can double-click to download the files from the manufacturer's websites. Double-click the AGFA PPDs URL file and the Tektronix PPDs URL file to download sets of PPD files for each company. If either of those URLs doesn't work, double-click the Adobe PPDs for Win.url file to access Adobe's download page for both printer drivers and PPDs. Once the files are downloaded, run the Agfa.exe and Tek.exe installer files, then use the Add Printer Wizard to add AGFA AccuSet 1500 and Tektronix Phaser 480X printers (uncheck the Automatically Detect And Install My Plug And Play Printer check box, and select the printer software manually).

List of Additional Files

Printed with each activity is a list of files students open to complete that activity. Many activities also require additional files that students do not open, but are needed to support the file(s) students are working with. These supporting files are included with the student data files on the course CD-ROM or data disk. Do not delete these files.

NOTES

LESSON 1

Creating PDFs from Technical Documents

Lesson Time
45 minutes

Lesson Objectives:

In this lesson, you will create PDFs from tcchnical documents.

You will:

- Generate a PDF version of a file from within Microsoft Office Visio.
- Generate a PDF version of a file from within AutoCAD.
- View and measure details in a technical drawing.

Introduction

As a workplace professional, you have created PDF documents from office documents. However, you may also need to generate PDF documents from complicated documents and drawings. In this lesson, you will convert existing technical documents into navigable PDF documents.

Complex technical documents often require additional attention when converting them into PDF documents. By setting the proper options during the PDF creation process, you can ensure that all elements of the original content are represented and viewable in the resulting PDF.

TOPIC A

Create PDF Documents from within Microsoft Visio

Like any other program in the Microsoft Office family, Visio's complex flow charts and processes can be converted to PDF documents. In this topic, you will create PDF documents from within Visio.

Visio is commonly used by planners and engineers to create diagrams, charts, schedules, sketches, and even complete technical drawings. Converting a Visio document to PDF enables others to view the technical documents without sacrificing layers of information in the process.

Layers

Definition:

A *layer* is an object used to display information in a PDF document. The name of the layers is listed on the Layers tab. The layers that appear in the PDF document are based on the layers created in the original application; you cannot create layers in Acrobat. However, you can view or hide a layer by clicking the Visibility column to the left of the layer in the Layers tab. You can also lock a layer to prevent users from making changes to that layer.

Example:

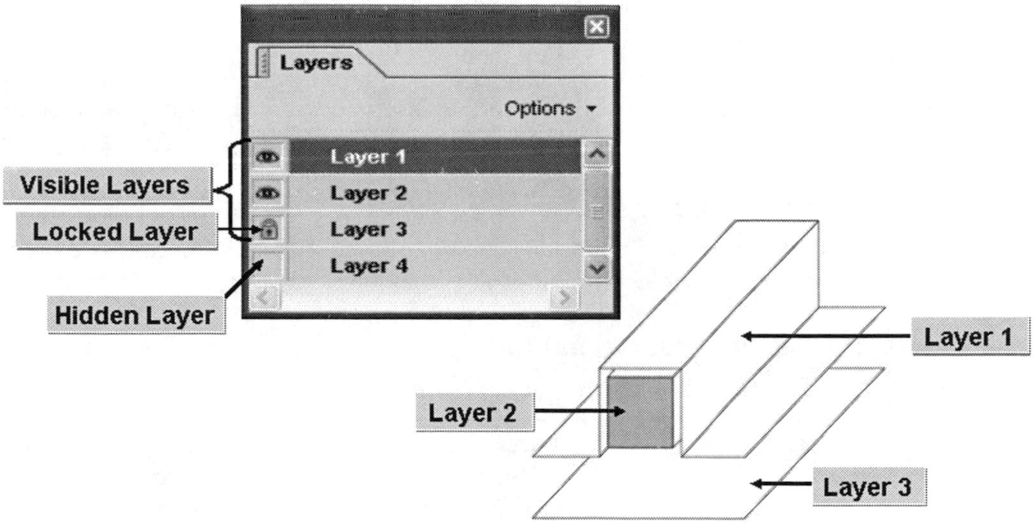

Layers Tab

The Layers tab provides a list of all layers in a document. You can use the Layers tab to change the properties of a layer. You can use this tab to rename a layer, set the default state of a layer, lock a layer, select the initial visibility, print, and export states of the layers.

How to Create PDF Documents from within Microsoft Visio

Procedure Reference: Create a PDF Version of a Document Using Microsoft Office Visio

To create a PDF version of a document using Microsoft Office Visio:

1. In Microsoft Visio, open the document you want to convert.
2. If you want to specify settings that control the generated PDF document's attributes, choose Adobe PDF→Change Conversion Settings. The Acrobat PDFMaker dialog box is displayed.
3. In the Settings tab, specify PDFMaker and application settings used to convert the file to PDF.
4. Specify settings in the Security tab.
5. Specify the appropriate settings in the Acrobat PDFMaker dialog box and click OK.
6. If you want to generate a PDF file that includes all the pages from the Visio file, then choose Adobe PDF→Convert All Pages In Drawing. A check mark is displayed next to that command when it is enabled.
7. Convert the document to a PDF document.
   - On the PDFMaker toolbar, click one of the Convert To Adobe PDF buttons;
   - Or, from the Adobe PDF menu, choose one of the Convert To Adobe PDF commands.

8. If the Acrobat PDFMaker dialog box is displayed, verify that the Include Custom Properties check box is checked and click Continue.

9. Select an option to determine whether to flatten or retain layers for the current page. Click Continue, and click Convert To Adobe PDF.

10. If the Save Adobe PDF File As dialog box is displayed, specify a name and location for the file, and then click Save.

PDFMaker Application Settings

You can use the Application Settings for Visio to control how the file is converted to PDF as explained in Table 1-1.

Table 1-1: *Settings options in Visio*

Settings Tab Option	Description
Attach Source File To Adobe PDF check box	Check this check box to attach the original Visio application file to the generated PDF file. An attachment icon will appear on the PDF document's first page, which you can double-click to open the attachment in its authoring application.
Add Links To Adobe PDF check box	Check this check box so that any links in the original document will also function in the PDF version of the file.
Add Bookmarks To Adobe PDF check box	Check this check box to generate a bookmark for each page of a multi-page Visio document.
Always Flatten Layers In Adobe PDF check box	Check this check box to create PDF files without layers that match the ones created in Visio. Uncheck it to include layers.
Open Layers Pane When Viewed In Acrobat check box	Check this check box to make the Layers pane appear automatically when a Visio document is converted to a layered PDF document.
Convert Comments To Adobe PDF Comments check box	Check this check box to convert comments in the Visio file to comments in the PDF file.

Activity 1-1

Converting Figures in a Microsoft Visio Document to PDF

Activity Time:

5 minutes

Data Files:

- Sample Panel and Cross-Section.vsd

1. You will need Microsoft Visio installed on your computer to complete this activity in full, but can open a sample PDF document created from Visio to perform step 2.

Scenario:

You are a senior engineer at Integix Products Group, a company that designs heating, ventilation, and air conditioning (HVAC) components and systems. You have created figures for the white paper in Microsoft Visio to be included in a PDF document. You divided the content of a composite drawing into layers, which you wish to retain in the PDF document so that viewers can view them individually, if desired.

What You Do	How You Do It
1. **Convert the Sample Panel and Cross-Section.vsd file, ensuring that all layers will be displayed in the PDF document.** If you don't have Microsoft Visio on your computer, open the Sample Panel and Cross-Section Complete.pdf document and skip to step 2.	a. **Choose Start→All Programs→Microsoft Office→Microsoft Office Visio 2003.** b. **Choose File→Open.** c. **Click My Computer.** d. **Navigate to the C:\084173Data\Technical Documents\Activity1\Start folder.** e. **Select the Sample Panel and Cross-Section.vsd file and click Open.** f. **Choose Adobe PDF→Change Conversion Settings.**

g. **Verify that the Always Flatten Layers In Adobe PDF check box is unchecked. Click OK.**

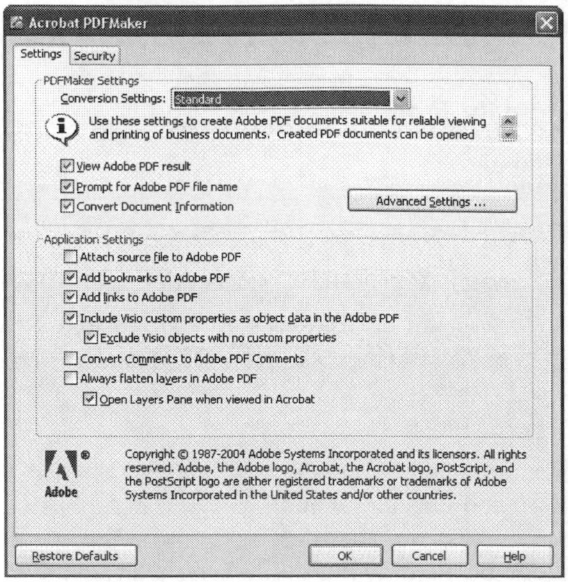

h. **Choose Adobe PDF→Convert All Pages In Drawing.**

i. **Choose Adobe PDF→Convert To Adobe PDF.**

j. In the Acrobat PDFMaker dialog box, **click Continue.**

k. **Select the Retain All Layers option and click Continue.**

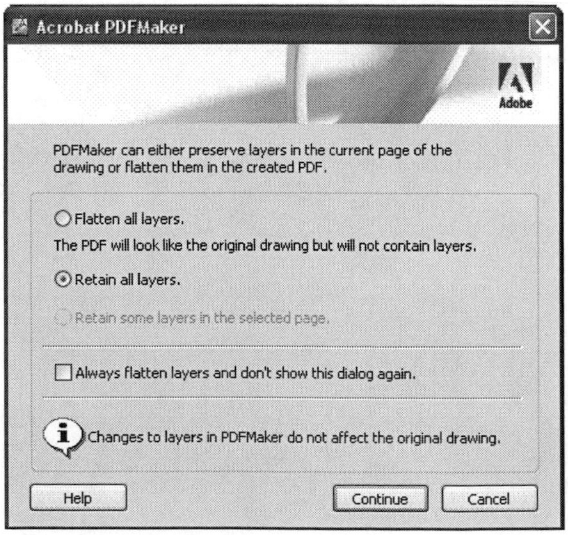

	l. **Click Convert To PDF.**
	m. The default file name in the File Name text box is the name of the original Visio file, with the pdf extension. **Click Save.**
	n. In the Document Status dialog box, **click Close.**
2. **Test the layers in the PDF file, showing only the ones applicable to each page.**	a. In the Layers pane, in the Visibility column to the left of the Honeycomb layer, **click the Eye icon** to make the contents of this layer disappear from the page.
	b. On the status bar, **click the Next Page button.**
	c. From the Options menu, **choose List Layers For Current Page.**
	d. On the status bar, **click the Previous Page button.**
	e. **Close the Adobe Acrobat Professional window.**

TOPIC B

Create PDF Documents from within Autodesk AutoCAD

Much like Visio documents, Autodesk AutoCAD files are complicated and difficult to share without giving up some detailed elements. In this topic, you will receive an overview of how to create a layered PDF document from an open AutoCAD document.

Many engineers create technical drawings with AutoCAD, the most commonly used computer-aided drawing program. From within AutoCAD, you can generate a PDF version that includes information and functionality based on elements of the original AutoCAD file.

Acrobat and AutoCAD

After you install Adobe Acrobat 7 using the default installation, you can use several methods to convert AutoCAD documents to the PDF format.

- Click one of the three Convert To Adobe PDF buttons to generate a PDF version of the current AutoCAD file.

- From the Adobe PDF menu, select a command to specify conversion settings and to generate PDF documents.
- In the AutoCAD command line, type PDF to generate a PDF version of the current file.

How to Create PDF Documents from within Autodesk AutoCAD

Procedure Reference: Create a PDF Version of a Document Using Autodesk AutoCAD

To create a PDF version of a document using Autodesk AutoCAD:

1. In AutoCAD, open the document you want to convert.
2. If you want to specify settings that control the generated PDF document's attributes, choose Adobe PDF→Change Conversion Settings. The Acrobat PDFMaker dialog box is displayed.
3. In the Settings tab, specify PDFMaker and application settings used to convert the file to PDF.
4. After specifying settings in the Acrobat PDFMaker dialog box, click OK.
5. Convert the document to a PDF document.
   - On the toolbar, click one of the Convert To Adobe PDF buttons;
   - Or, from the Adobe PDF menu, choose one of the Convert To Adobe PDF commands;
   - Or, in the AutoCAD command line, type PDF.
6. If you specified that the AutoCAD layers should not be flattened, you can specify which layers from the AutoCAD file are included in the generated PDF document. In the Acrobat PDFMaker (Convert To Adobe PDF) dialog box, choose settings for mapping AutoCAD layers to Acrobat layers.
   a. From the Named Layer Filters drop-down list, select the AutoCAD layers you want to display in the Layers In Drawing list box within the dialog box.
   b. If you want to change how the layers are sorted in the Layers In Drawing list box, click a column heading.
   c. To select the AutoCAD layers you want to add to the PDF version of the document, click a layer name in the Layers In Drawing list box, then hold down Ctrl, and click additional layers you want to add. You can also right-click within the list box and choose Select All.
   d. Click the Add Layer(s) button to move the selected layers to the Layers In PDF list box, or click the Create Layer Set button to move the selected layers to the Layers In PDF list box as a layer set.
   e. If you want to be able to control a layer's visibility in the PDF file, in the Layers In PDF list box, uncheck the Locked On check box next to that layer. Checking the Locked On check box makes that layer visible in the PDF file always.
   f. Once the layers are set up the way you want, you can save the current layer configuration so you can load it again by clicking the Add PDF Setting button.

g. Click the Convert To PDF button to generate the PDF file with the layers you specified.

7. If you want to change the default viewing state of a layer in Acrobat, right-click the layer and choose Properties. From the Default State drop-down list, select On or Off to specify whether the layer is visible or hidden by default.

Application Settings for AutoCAD

You can use the Application Settings for AutoCAD to control how the file is converted to PDF as explained in Table 1-2.

Table 1-2: *Settings options in AutoCAD*

Settings Tab Option	Description
Attach Source File To Adobe PDF check box	Check this check box to attach the original AutoCAD application file to the generated PDF file. An attachment icon will appear on the PDF document's first page, which you can double-click to open the attachment in its authoring application.
Add Links To Adobe PDF check box	Check this check box so that any links in the original document will also function in the PDF version of the file.
Add Bookmarks To Adobe PDF check box	Check this check box to allow specific components within a document to be converted to bookmarks in the PDF version.
Always Flatten Layers In Adobe PDF check box	Check this check box to create PDF files that do not include layers from the AutoCAD document. Uncheck it to include layers.
Open Layers Pane When Viewed In Acrobat check box	Check this check box to make the Layers pane appear automatically when an AutoCAD document is converted to a layered PDF document.

ACTIVITY 1-2

Converting an AutoCAD File to PDF

Activity Time:

5 minutes

Scenario:

You want to explore the different options available in AutoCAD for converting documents to the PDF format.

What You Do	How You Do It

1. **What are the additional components installed in AutoCAD during a default installation of Adobe Acrobat Professional?**

    a) The Adobe PDF menu and the Convert From AutoCAD buttons.

    b) The Convert To PDF buttons and the Adobe PDF menu.

    c) The Convert To PDF From AutoCAD buttons and the Adobe PDF menu.

    d) The Adobe PDF menu and the Convert PDF buttons.

2. **How can you change the settings specified for converting AutoCAD documents to the PDF format?**

3. **How can you convert an AutoCAD document to PDF?**

Topic C

Measure Technical Drawing Content

Another important aspect of accessing information in technical PDF documents is the ability to view detailed technical drawings. In this topic, you will quickly locate and measure specific information.

Technical drawings are designed for printing or plotting on very large paper and they often contain multiple layers of very detailed information. This combination of attributes could make a technical drawing much more difficult to work with on screen than its hard copy. Acrobat offers tools and interfaces to quickly display the smallest detail and to measure distances and areas of importance.

Loupe Tool

The Loupe tool lets you view a specific portion of the PDF document at a higher magnification within a small window. This tool is especially useful to zoom in to see fine details in the document.

Pan & Zoom Window

When you select Pan & Zoom Window on the Zoom toolbar, the Pan & Zoom window is displayed. You can resize and reposition the box within the window to zoom and scroll through the content in the Document pane.

Measuring Toolbar

The Measuring toolbar helps you measure distances, perimeters, and areas of objects in PDF documents. The elements on the Measuring toolbar are shown in Figure 1-1.

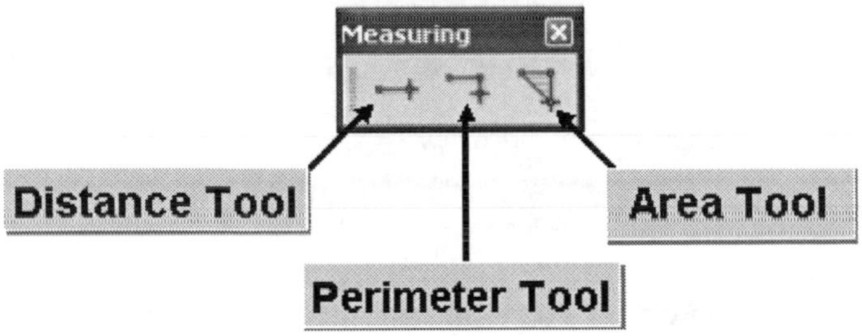

Figure 1-1: *Elements on the Measuring toolbar*

How to Measure Technical Drawing Content

Procedure Reference: Control Layer Visibility

To display or hide specific layers in a layered PDF document:

1. In the navigation pane, select the Layers tab to view it.

Changing the visibility of layers and then saving the document does not save these changes. To change a layer's default visibility when the file is opened, right-click the layer name, choose Properties and then from the Default State drop-down list, select On or Off.

2. If you want to hide a layer's contents, in the Visibility column to the left of the layer, click the Eye icon.
3. If you want to show a hidden layer's contents, click in the Visibility column so that the Eye icon reappears.
4. If the document contains layer sets, click the plus (+) or minus (–) icon next to the layer set name to expand or collapse the layers grouped under it.

Procedure Reference: View Detailed Information in a Document with Large Pages

To view details in a large technical drawing:

1. If you want to display two views of a single document at once, choose Window→Split to display the current PDF document in two separate panes. You can then scroll, change the magnification, change layer visibility, and navigate among pages in either pane without changing the view of the document in the other pane. Adjust the space allocated between the panes by dragging the splitter bar that is displayed between them.

   When you finish viewing a document using split panes, choose Window→Split to return to a single pane.

2. If you want to pan and zoom large document pages containing technical drawing content, use the Pan & Zoom window, the Loupe tool, and/or the Dynamic Zoom tool to efficiently and dynamically view the content you need to see.
3. If you want to view window content flipped 90 degrees, choose View→Rotate View→Clockwise or choose View→Rotate View→Counterclockwise to rotate the drawing by 90 degrees. Any Loupe window contents rotate about the loupe point selected, so the contents in the middle will not rotate out of view.

Procedure Reference: Measure Distances and Areas in Scale Drawings

To measure distances, perimeters, and areas in a scale drawing:

1. Choose Tools→Measuring→Show Measuring Toolbar to display the Measuring toolbar.
2. Select the tool for the type of measurement you want, and click in the drawing to create endpoints of segments. The measurement is displayed in the Tool dialog box, which is displayed automatically.
3. In the Tool dialog box, enter the scale of the drawing. For example, if the drawing designates that the scale is 1/8" = 1 foot, specify information in the text boxes and drop-down lists in the dialog box.
4. If you want the measurement lines you create to remain visible as a comment, check the Annotate check box in the dialog box before adding the lines. Otherwise, the measurement lines you draw will disappear when you select another tool or create another measurement.

When you position the Hand tool on a measurement object saved as a comment, a tooltip appears, displaying the measurement of the line or object.

Measurement Tools

You can use the measurement tools to determine the distances or areas in a document as shown in Table 1-3.

Table 1-3: *Tools on the Measuring toolbar*

Tool	Description
Distance tool	Click in two places to measure the distance between those points.
Perimeter tool	Click in at least three places and then double-click to create the last point (or click the last point you have already created) to measure the combined distance of the segments you create.
Area tool	Click in at least three places, then return to the first point, and click to close the polygon shape to measure the area within the polygon you create.

ACTIVITY 1-3

Viewing and Measuring Information in a Floor Plan

Activity Time:

15 minutes

Data Files:

- FloorPlan.pdf

Scenario:

You are a senior design engineer at Pellick Design Group, a company that designs and contracts building projects. One of your group members has given you FloorPlan.pdf, a PDF document created from an AutoCAD drawing of a building floor plan. You need to quickly check some of the drawing's details before you approve it. You need to generate a material take-off for the building, so you want to measure the perimeter of the building, designated by cloud notation in Figure 1-2.

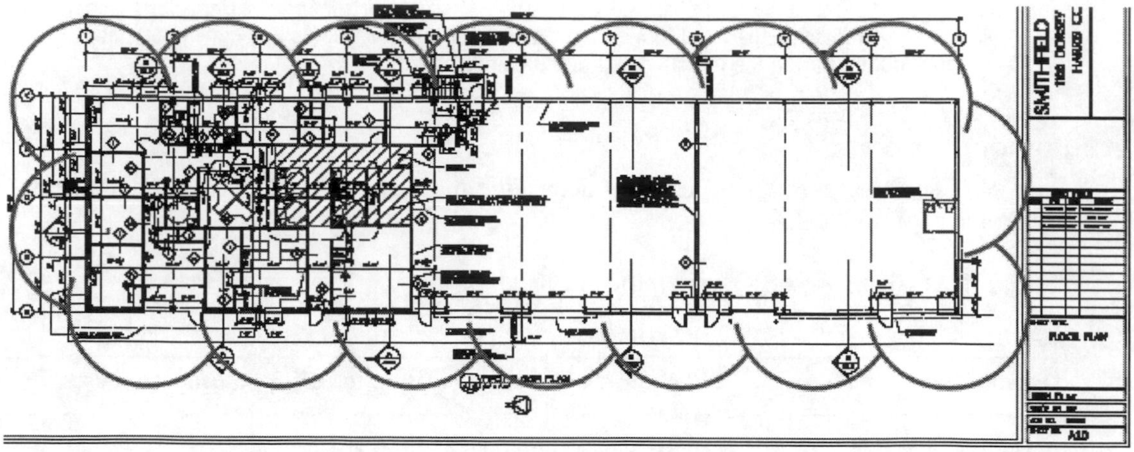

Figure 1-2: *You want to measure the approximate perimeter of this building.*

What You Do	How You Do It
1. **View the FloorPlan.pdf document in multiple panes, with one pane displaying an overview of the floor plan at the Fit Page view and another displaying a more detailed view.**	a. **Choose Window→Split** to split the document pane into two. b. On the Zoom toolbar, **click the Fit Page button** to display the entire page in the top portion of the document pane. c. **Click anywhere in the bottom portion of the document pane** to bring focus to that portion. d. On the Zoom toolbar, from the Magnification drop-down list, **select 25%.** e. **Drag the divider between the panes up by an inch** so that the top portion appears small and the bottom one appears large. 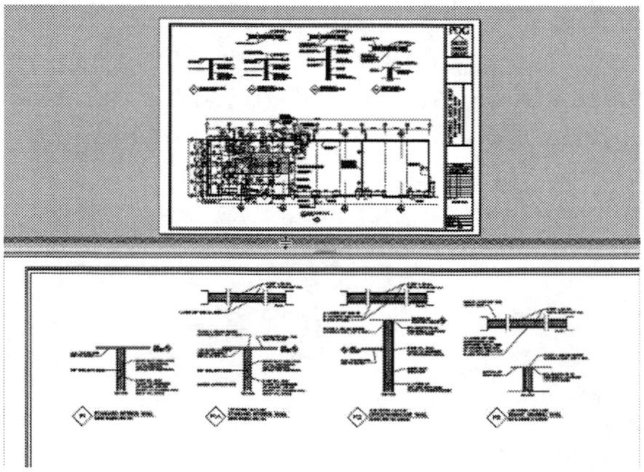

2. **Dynamically zoom in on the text to the right of the third diamond annotation, which is labeled P2, until the top line is large enough to be legible.**

   a. On the Zoom toolbar, **click the arrow next to the Zoom In tool.**

   b. **Select the Dynamic Zoom tool.**

   c. In the bottom portion of the document pane, **position the mouse pointer below and to the right of the third diamond from the left and then drag up and to the left** so that you can read the words "separates office from warehouse" under "OFFICE/WAREHOUSE WALL" comfortably.

3. **Pan and zoom the bottom portion of the document pane so the entire height of the office building's left side, which is the bottom-left side of the drawing, is visible.**

   a. **Choose Tools→Zoom→Pan & Zoom Window.**

   b. In the Pan & Zoom window, **drag the red box by its center to the bottom-left side of the drawing.**

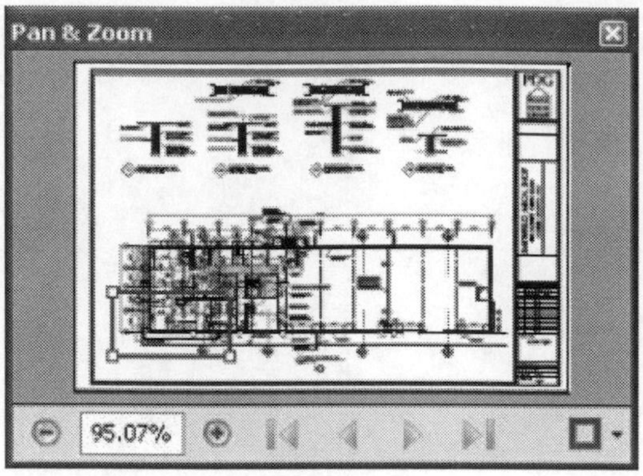

   c. **Move the Pan & Zoom window over the Layers pane.**

   d. In the Pan & Zoom window, **drag the top-right handle of the red box to make the red box approximately the height of the building.**

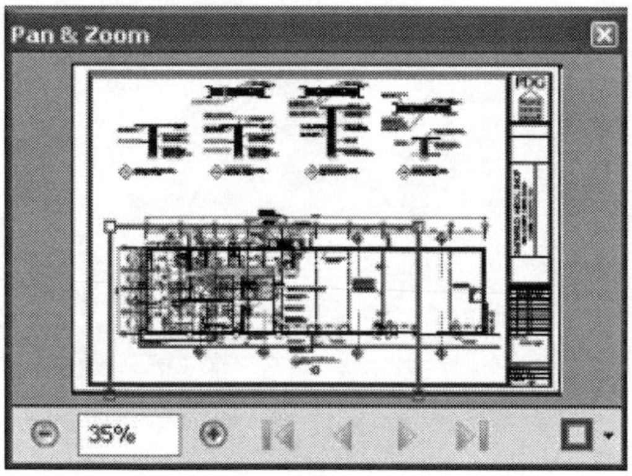

   e. **Close the Pan & Zoom window.**

---

4. **Hide the layers that clutter the view of the room layout.**

   a. On the Basic toolbar, **select the Hand tool.**

   b. In the Layers pane, in the Visibility column to the left of the Wall Details layer set, **click the Eye icon.**

c. In the Layers pane, **collapse the Wall Details layer set.**

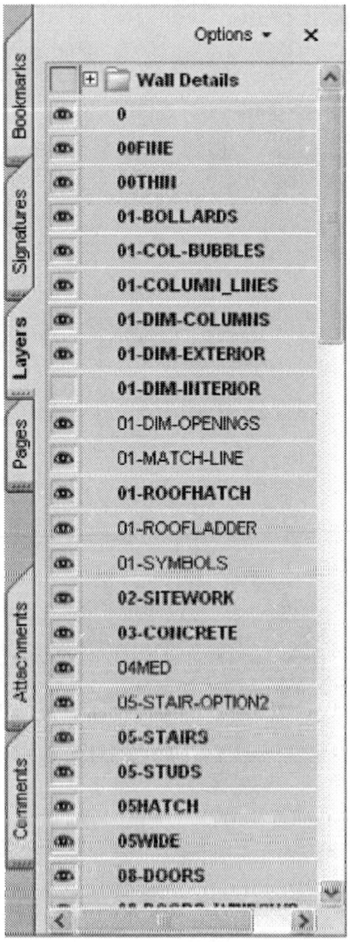

d. In the Layers pane, in the Visibility column to the left of the 01-DIM-INTERIOR layer, **click the Eye icon.**

e. In the Layers pane, **scroll down to view the A-Anno-Panl layer.**

f. In the Layers pane, in the Visibility column to the left of the A-Anno-Panl layer, **click the Eye icon.**

g. In the Layers pane, in the Visibility column to the left of the A-DETL-IDEN layer, **click the Eye icon.**

5. **View the dimensions and small text surrounding the circled letter C at 125% magnification while retaining the magnification in both portions of the document pane.**

a. On the Zoom toolbar, **click the arrow next to the Dynamic Zoom tool.**

b. **Select the Loupe tool.**

c. In the bottom portion of the document pane, **click the circled letter C.**

d. In the Loupe Tool window, **click the - button two times** to view at 125%.

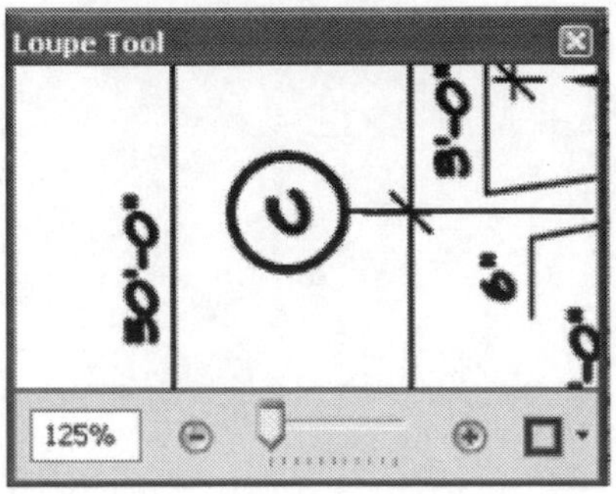

e. **Move the Loupe Tool window over the Layers pane, and drag the bottom-right handle of the window to increase its size** so that the text to the right is visible.

f. In the bottom portion of the document pane, **click slightly to the right of the circled letter C** to center the words "Sanitary Sewer" within the Loupe Tool window.

---

6. **Rotate the page 90° clockwise to make the vertical text on either side of the circled letter B easier to read, and rotate it back to its normal orientation.**

a. **Choose View→Rotate View→Clockwise.**

b. In the bottom portion of the document pane, **click the circled letter B.**

c. **Choose View→Rotate View→Counterclockwise.**

d. **Close the Loupe window.**

---

7. **Measure the perimeter of the building in square feet.**

a. On the Basic toolbar, **select the Hand tool.**

b. **Choose Tools→Zoom→Pan & Zoom Window.**

c. In the Pan & Zoom window, **drag the red box by its center to the bottom-left side of the drawing.**

d. In the Pan & Zoom window, **drag the top-right handle of the red box as necessary** to view the building's width and height in the bottom portion of the document pane.

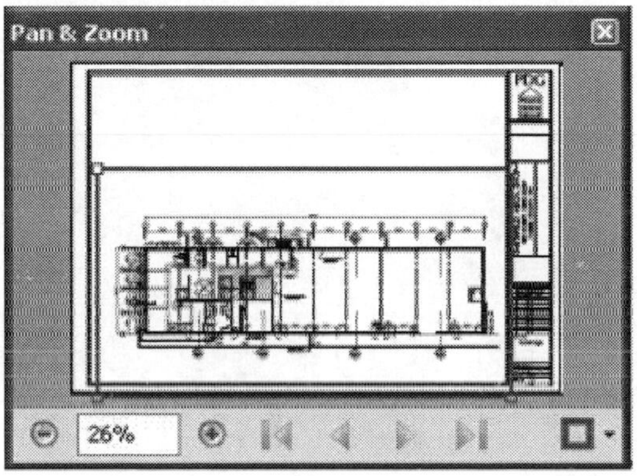

e. **Choose Tools→Measuring→Show Measuring Toolbar.**

f. On the Measuring toolbar, **select the Perimeter tool.**

g. **If necessary, move the Perimeter Tool window to the right of the document pane.**

h. On the Perimeter Tool dialog box, **double-click in the first Scale Ratio text box from the left and type *0.125***

i. On the Perimeter Tool dialog box, **from the drop-down list at the right corner, select Ft.**

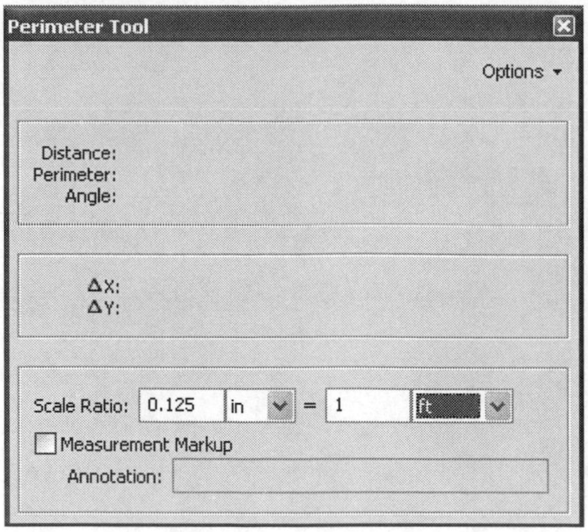

j. In the bottom portion of the document pane, **click the top-left corner of the building.**

k. In the bottom portion of the document pane, **click the top-right corner, then the bottom-right, then the bottom-left corners of the building.**

l. **Position the mouse pointer accurately on the first point you clicked, and double-click.**

m. The Perimeter Tool dialog box displays the value of the perimeter in feet. **Close the Perimeter Tool window.**

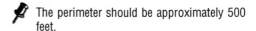

The perimeter should be approximately 500 feet.

n. **Close the Pan & Zoom window, the Measuring toolbar, and the FloorPlan.pdf file.**

Lesson 1 Follow-up

In this lesson, you converted technical documents from several applications to PDFs. By setting the proper options during the PDF creation process, you can ensure that all elements of the original content are represented and viewable in the resulting PDF.

1. **Why do you want to convert your documents to PDF?**

2. **Which of the tools you learned in this lesson will you use to measure technical drawings? Why?**

NOTES

LESSON 2

Enhancing PDF Documents

Lesson Time
85 minutes

Lesson Objectives:

In this lesson, you will enhance the utility and accessibility of PDF documents.

You will:

- Embed multimedia in a PDF document.
- Create actions in a PDF document.
- Optimize PDF files.
- Batch process PDF documents.
- Make a PDF document more accessible.
- Create structured PDF documents.

Introduction

Creating PDF documents is only part of making them useful. Beyond adding navigation elements, you can further enhance your PDFs. In this lesson, you will enhance PDFs so that they are more useful to your desired audience.

By enhancing the quality and utility of your PDFs with additional features, you can make the content more available to a wider audience.

TOPIC A

Embed Multimedia

PDF documents can use content that is unavailable in printed documents. In this lesson, you will embed multimedia elements to make a PDF document more engaging to the viewer.

Adding multimedia to an electronically distributed PDF file can help the document convey information more effectively in a way that would be impossible in a printed document. It can add not only aesthetic value, increasing the viewer's interest, but can also add content, such as a video explaining how to install a product, which would be impossible to include in a "static" print document.

Media Types that Can Be Embedded

Acrobat 7 uses media players installed on your computer to play video and sound files. It can play files compatible with the following players:

- Apple QuickTime Player
- Macromedia Flash Player
- Windows Built-In Player
- RealOne Player
- Windows Media Player

Media Properties

Using the Settings tab in the Multimedia Properties dialog box, you can specify the title of the movie, a description of the media file, and rendition media settings, such as player controls and volume level. You can also determine the border appearance of the play area, change the poster that appears in it, and define new actions for various mouse movements.

How to Embed Multimedia

Procedure Reference: Add a Media Clip to a PDF Document

To add a media clip to a PDF document:

1. Select the tool for the clip type you want to add.
    - Select the Movie tool or the Sound tool from the Advanced Editing toolbar;

- Or, choose Tools→Advanced Editing→Movie Tool, or Tools→Advanced Editing→Sound Tool.

2. Display the Add Movie or Add Sound dialog box.
   - Double-click the page where you want the top-left corner of the clip's play area;
   - Or, click and drag to specify the clip's play area.
3. Select the media compatibility option.
   - The Acrobat 6 (And Later) Compatible Media option requires the viewer to use Acrobat or Adobe Reader 6 or later versions.
   - The Acrobat 5 (And Earlier) Compatible Media option allows the viewer to use Acrobat or Adobe Reader 5 or previous versions.
4. Specify the media clip by typing its name or by clicking Browse and navigating to it.
5. If you initially dragged instead of double-clicked to specify the location of the clip's play area on the page, check the Snap To Content Proportions check box to prevent the movie from appearing stretched in one direction.
6. Choose a poster setting to determine what still media should appear as a "placeholder" for the movie or sound clip when it's not playing.
7. If you selected the Acrobat 6 (And Later) Compatible Media option, choose a content type from the Content Type drop-down list if you want Acrobat to use a different media player than the default.
8. Click OK.

Media Compatibility Options

There are two kinds of media compatibility options available in the Add Movie and Add Sound dialog boxes. The Acrobat 6 (And Later) Compatible Media option allows for more flexibility, such as the ability to embed the media in the PDF file rather than linking to an external file. It also allows for multiple renditions of the file to be played, depending on the viewer's settings. For example, if the user does not have the viewer software (such as QuickTime) for the default media, the PDF could load a different rendition (such as an .avi file) created for use with another media player. Or, it could download a smaller version of the file for a slower computer, or even render subtitles in the appropriate language.

The Acrobat 5 (And Earlier) Compatible Media option allows fewer playback and content type options than the Acrobat 6 (And Later) Compatible Media option. However, it cannot embed media, or play many formats, such as Flash files, which are available to Acrobat 6.

Procedure Reference: Manipulate the Media Clip on the Page

To manipulate a media clip on the page:

1. Select the media clip with either the tool used to create it or the Select Object tool (all in the Advanced Editing toolbar).
2. If you want to move the clip, drag anywhere inside it.
3. If you want to resize the clip, drag one of its corners, holding down Shift to retain its original height-to-width proportion.

4. If you want to delete the clip, click it and press Delete.

Procedure Reference: Specify Media Properties

To change media properties:

1. Display the Multimedia Properties dialog box.
    - Double-click the media clip with either the tool used to create it or the Select Object tool (all in the Advanced Editing toolbar);
    - Or, right-click the media clip and choose Properties from the shortcut menu.
2. Specify properties (the ones available depend on whether or not you selected the Acrobat 6 (And Later) Compatible Media option when adding the media clip).
3. Click Close.

ACTIVITY 2-1

Adding a Movie to a PDF Document

Activity Time:

10 minutes

Data Files:

- Cyclingdatasheet.pdf
- mountainbike.avi

Scenario:

You are working as a graphic designer for a design firm, Super Fast Wheels. You have been given a Cyclingdatasheet.pdf document for review, which was converted from HTML pages. You feel that the Cycling page can be made more interesting. So you have developed a short, fast-loading video clip showing the bike in action. You want to allow the viewers to see the video when they are not connected to the Internet, and without having to download multiple files.

What You Do	How You Do It
1. **True or False? You could use either Acrobat 6 or Acrobat 5 compatibility to achieve the objectives for the movie clip you are adding.** __ True __ False	

2. **Add the mountainbike.avi file to the Cycling page.**

a. On the Advanced Editing toolbar, **select the Movie tool.**

b. **Scroll to page 2.**

c. **Double-click beneath the image to the left of the page.**

d. **Click Browse.**

e. **Select mountainbike.avi and click Select.**

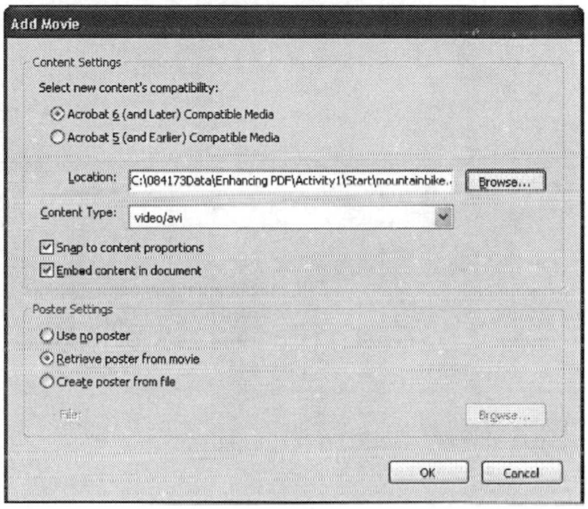

f. **Click OK.**

3. **Position and resize the video clip to fit to the left of the document text and play the video.**

   a. **Drag the movie by the center so its bottom edge aligns with the black border at the end of the page.**

   b. **Click and drag the top-right selection handle towards the center of the image till the right edge of the avi file aligns with the right edge of the image above it.**

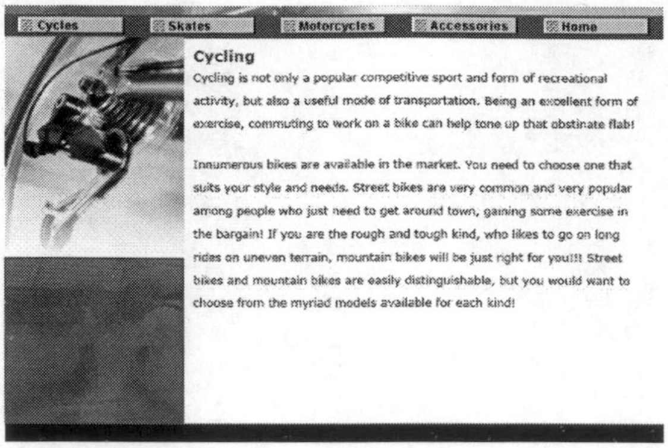

   c. On the Basic toolbar, **select the Hand tool.**

   d. **Click the movie** to play it.

   e. In the Manage Trust For Multimedia Content dialog box, **select the second option and click Play.**

4. **Lower the playback volume of the video, then play the video.**

a. On the Advanced Editing toolbar, **select the Movie tool.**

b. **Double-click the video clip.**

c. **Select Rendition From Mountainbike.avi and click Edit Rendition.**

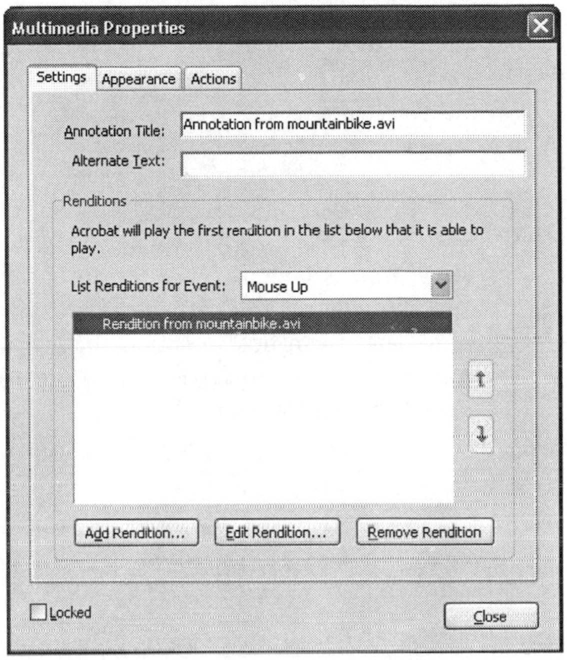

d. **Select the Playback Settings tab.**

e. **Double-click in the Volume text box and type *60***

f. **Click OK.**

g. **Click Close.**

h. On the Basic toolbar, **select the Hand tool.**

i. **Click the movie** to play it.

j. **Save the document.**

TOPIC B

Create Actions

A well-designed PDF document can contain elements that can be used to direct the attention of the user to specific content. In this topic, you will create actions in a PDF that enhance the document's usability.

Actions enable your audience to concentrate on the content rather than the document's interface.

Actions

Definition:

An *action* is a step you set up to occur automatically when the PDF file encounters a specific trigger. You can assign actions to bookmarks, pages, links, buttons, media clips, and form fields. Actions include controlling media or running JavaScript code, and can respond to a wide variety of triggers. Additionally, you may assign multiple actions to one trigger.

Example:

Action Triggers

You can assign actions to the following triggers, and they occur in this order of precedence if more than one occurs at once:

- **Mouse Up** Triggers when the mouse button is released at the end of a click. You should use this instead of Mouse Down, so the user can move the mouse away from the object after pressing the mouse button down if they decide not to click it.
- **Page Visible** Triggers when the specified page appears, whether or not it's the current page (for example, it may be the second page in a side-by-side layout).
- **Page Invisible** Triggers when the specified page is no longer visible.
- **Page Enter** Triggers when the specified page becomes the current page.

- **Page Exit** Triggers when the user goes to another page.
- **Mouse Down** Triggers when the mouse button is pressed (prior to being released).
- **Mouse Enter** Triggers when the mouse pointer enters the object (a field or media clip's play area).
- **Mouse Exit** Triggers when the mouse pointer leaves the object (a field or media clip's play area).
- **On Receive Focus** Triggers when the form field receives focus, either by the user clicking in it or tabbing to it.
- **On Lose Focus** Triggers when the user moves the focus to a different form field.

Assignable Actions

You can assign the following actions to bookmarks, pages, links, buttons, media clips, and form fields:

- **Execute A Menu Item** Executes a specified menu command as the action.
- **Go To A 3D View** Changes the view of the document to the specified view.
- **Go To A Page View** After you use the Snapshot tool to copy an area of the PDF document to the clipboard, you can define an action that jumps to that area.
- **Import Form Data** Places data from another file into the active form.
- **Open A File** Launches and opens a file.
- **Open A Web Link** You can link to http, ftp, and mailto protocols to open web pages, FTP sites, and send email.
- **Play A Sound** Plays the specified sound file.
- **Play Media (Acrobat 5 Compatible)** Plays the specified movie that was created as Acrobat 5-compatible. There must already be a link to the movie in the PDF document for you to be able to select it.
- **Play Media (Acrobat 6 Later Compatible)** Plays the specified movie that was created as Acrobat 6-compatible. There must already be a link to the movie in the PDF document for you to be able to select it.
- **Read An Article** Follows an article thread in the active document or in another PDF document.
- **Reset A Form** Clears form data.
- **Run A JavaScript** Runs the specified JavaScript.
- **Set Layer Visibility** In a layered document, this specifies which layer settings are active.
- **Show/Hide A Field** This can make a field appear only under certain circumstances, such as a field that appears only when certain other fields are filled in. It can also create a "disjoint rollover" effect when applied to the Mouse Enter and Mouse Exit triggers of another object.
- **Submit A Form** Sends a form to a specific URL.

How to Create Actions

Procedure Reference: Assign an Action to an Object

To assign an action to an object:

1. Select the object to which you want to assign the action.
    - Select a bookmark by clicking its icon in the Bookmarks panel.
    - Select a page by clicking its thumbnail in the Pages panel.
    - Select a link with the Link tool or the Select Object tool.
    - Select a media clip with the appropriate media tool or the Select Object tool.
    - Select a button with the Button tool or the Select Object tool.
    - Select a form field with the appropriate form field tool or the Select Object tool.
2. Open the Properties dialog box.
    - Right-click the object and choose Properties;
    - Or, double-click the object.
3. Select the Actions tab.
4. From the Select Trigger drop-down list, select the trigger action when applicable (you cannot set a trigger for bookmarks and links, which are always activated by a mouse click).
5. From the Select Action drop-down list, select the action type to occur when the trigger is activated, and click Add.
6. If desired, click Edit, and change the action settings.
7. If you add multiple actions to an object, they occur in the order they appear; you can select an action and click the Up or Down button to change the sequence.
8. Click Close.

ACTIVITY 2-2

Adding Actions to View Media in a PDF Document

Activity Time:

5 minutes

Data Files:

- Cyclingdatasheet.pdf

1. Display the file at 60% magnification level

Scenario:

You are concerned that people won't take the time to view the media clip you added to the Cycling page of the interactive data sheet if they have to click it themselves. Similarly, while the Flash animation on the opening page adds some visual interest, it only plays the first time the page is accessed. You want to make the media play automatically whenever the pages containing the multimedia content appear.

What You Do	How You Do It
1. **Add an action to page 2 of the Cyclingdatasheet.pdf document to make the video clip play automatically when the page opens.**	a. **Scroll up to page 1 in the Cyclingdatasheet.pdf document.**
	b. **Select the Pages tab.**
	c. **Right-click the page 2 thumbnail and choose Page Properties.**
	d. **Select the Actions tab.**
	e. **Verify that Page Open is selected from the Select Trigger drop-down list.** From the Select Action drop-down list, **select Play Media (Acrobat 6 And Later Compatible) and click Add.**

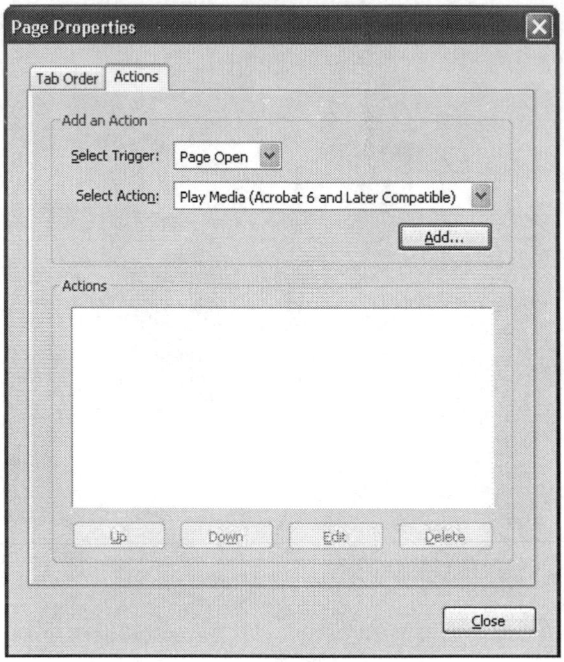

	f. **Select Annotation From Mountainbike.avi.**
	g. **Click OK and click Close.**
	h. In the document, **click the Cycles link.**

2. **Add an action to page 1 of the Cyclingdatasheet.pdf document to make the Flash animation play from the beginning when the page opens. Test the action, and close the document.**

a. In the Pages panel, **right-click the page 1 thumbnail and choose Page Properties.**

b. In the Actions tab, **verify that Page Open is selected from the Select Trigger drop-down list and Play Media (Acrobat 6 And Later Compatible) is selected from the Select Action drop-down list. Click Add.**

c. From the Operation To Perform drop-down list, **select Play From Beginning.**

d. **Select Annotation From Banner.swf.**

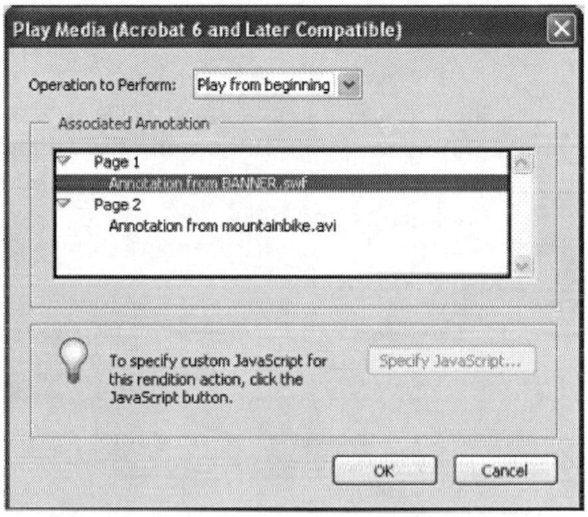

e. **Click OK and click Close.**

f. **Click the Home link in the document's navigation bar** to jump to page 1 and view the Flash animation play automatically.

g. In the Manage Trust For Multimedia Content dialog box, **select the second option and click Play** to jump to page 1 and watch the video play automatically.

h. **Save and close the document.**

TOPIC C

Optimize PDF Files

You have a PDF document to be distributed electronically and you want to keep the file size as small as possible. In this topic, you will optimize a PDF.

It can be frustrating to wait online for large files to download. If the wait is too long, people may choose to cancel the download. Reducing file sizes of PDF documents you generate means that the documents will take less time to transfer via email and the web.

PDF Optimizer

Definition:

PDF Optimizer is a command that is used to minimize PDF file size by compressing the file and its constituent parts so that it can be viewed quickly by the end user. The preferences you use to optimize a PDF file may vary depending on the mode of distribution—Internet or print. The elements of an optimized PDF document, such as bookmarks and links, function as before.

Example:

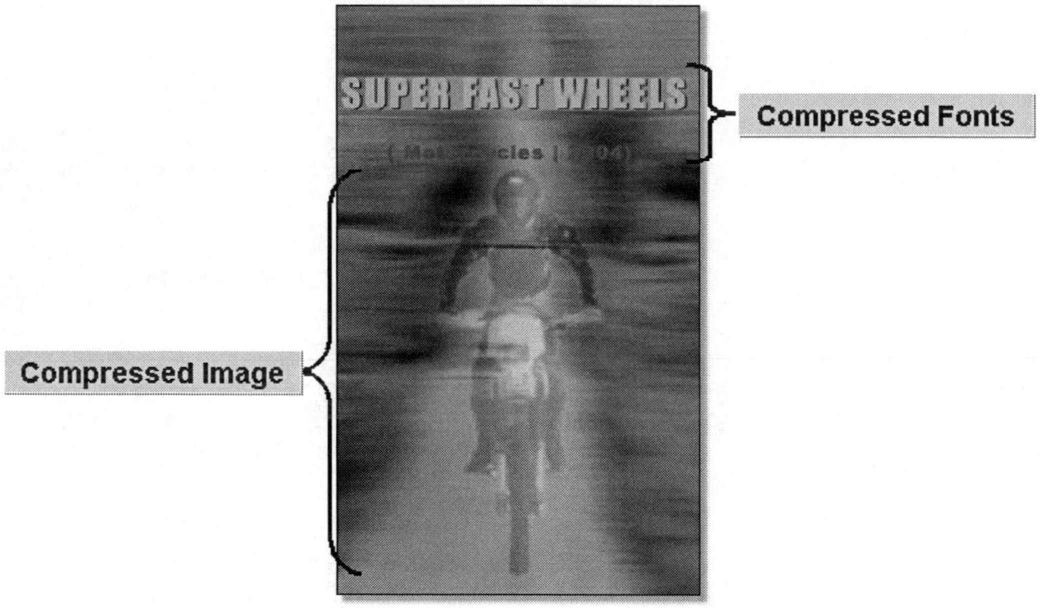

PDF Optimizer Options

The PDF Optimizer dialog box displays several options for optimizing a PDF.

- The Images panel lets you to set options for color, grayscale, and monochrome image compression.
- The Scanned Page panel lets you balance file size and quality based on the color content in the document and apply filters.

- The Fonts panel lets you embed and unembed fonts. If you know that the fonts used in the your PDF document are already installed on the computers of the people who will use it, you can unembed those fonts. If you unembed a font that is not available to someone reading your PDF document, Acrobat will display a substitute font when the document is opened on their computer.
- The Transparency panel lets you set transparency and flattener settings.
- The Discard Objects panel lets you specify objects that you want to remove from the PDF document and convert smooth lines to curves.
- The Clean Up panel lets you select an object conversion option and remove elements from the PDF document that you do not need.

How to Optimize PDF Files

Procedure Reference: Reduce a PDF Document's File Size by Optimizing It

To reduce a PDF document's file size by optimizing it:

1. Choose Advanced→PDF Optimizer. The PDF Optimizer dialog box is displayed.
2. If you want to change the compatibility of the document to make it readable in older versions of Acrobat, select an option from the Make Compatible With drop-down list.
3. If you want to see how each document element type contributes to the file size, click Audit Space Usage.
4. In the Images panel, you can select options to reduce the size of images by downsampling or compressing them.
5. In the Fonts panel, you can choose to unembed fonts that you expect the user to have on the computer that they use to view the document.
6. In the Clean Up panel, you can select a compression option, and can check the check boxes for items you can safely remove or discard from the file.
7. Click OK, and save the optimized document as a new file or overwrite the existing one.

ACTIVITY 2-3

Optimizing the Bike Catalog Document for Online Distribution

Activity Time:

5 minutes

Data Files:

- bikecatalog2004.pdf

Scenario:

You have been given the company's bike catalog, the bikecatalog2004.pdf file, but are suspicious that the file size is now larger than it needs to be. Because you are distributing it through the web, you want to reduce its size, keeping download time to a minimum. Since typical monitors are of 100 pixels per inch or lower resolution, you will limit the color and grayscale images to that value, so they will look reasonable at 100% magnification.

What You Do	How You Do It
1. **Optimize the bike catalog by limiting the color and grayscale resolution to 100 ppi.**	a. **Choose Advanced→PDF Optimizer.**
	b. **Click Audit Space Usage.**
	c. **View the total file size and element sizes and click OK.**
	d. In the Color Images section, **double-click in the Bicubic Downsampling To text box and type *100***
	e. In the Grayscale Images section, **double-click in the Bicubic Downsampling To text box and type *100***

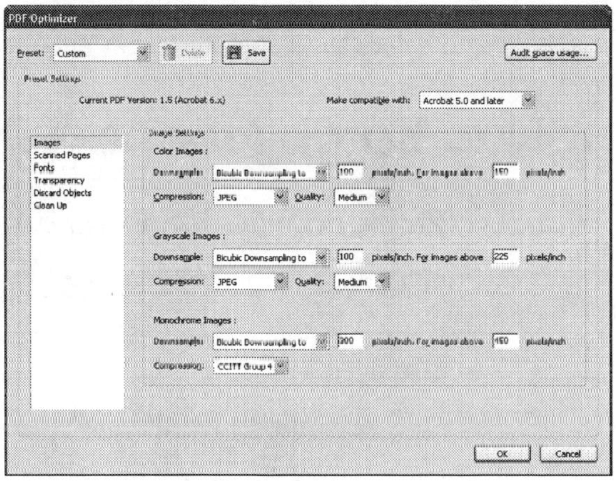

	f. **Click OK.**
	g. In the File Name text box, **type *bikecatalog2004web.pdf* and click Save.**
	h. **Page through the document to examine it, clicking links and bookmarks to verify that they still work.** The pages and graphics all look and behave identically to the way they were prior to optimizing.
	i. **Open the Bookmarks panel.**
	j. In the Bookmarks panel, **click the Sports bookmark** to verify that the bookmarks still work.

TOPIC D

Batch Process PDF Documents

Before you distribute PDF documents electronically, you may need to prepare several documents the same way at the same time. In this topic, you will use Acrobat to batch process multiple documents.

When performing actions repeatedly, a person may eventually make a mistake or forget a part of the required process. In contrast, setting up the computer to do "busy work" ensures accurate, consistent, and fast results, giving you more time to spend on creative design.

Batch Process

Batch processing is a feature that allows many files to be manipulated and processed as a group. This saves a lot of time. You can use the predefined batch sequences listed in the Batch Sequences dialog box or create a new sequence. You also have the option to edit a batch sequence and select the commands that need to be executed when a sequence is run.

How to Batch Process PDF Documents

Procedure Reference: Run an Existing Batch Sequence

To run an existing batch sequence:

1. Choose Advanced→Batch Processing. The Batch Sequences dialog box is displayed.
2. Select the process you want to run.
3. Click Run Sequence.
4. In the Run Sequence Confirmation dialog box, click OK. The Select Files to Process dialog box is displayed.
5. Select the files you want to process, and click Select. These files must be in the same folder in Windows.
6. If a message appears asking for additional input for a command within the sequence, select the options you want and click OK.
7. When the Progress dialog box disappears, the sequence has finished running, and you can click Close.

Procedure Reference: Create a Batch Sequence

To create a custom batch sequence:

1. Choose Advanced→Batch Processing.

   To edit an existing sequence, use the same steps as listed here, but select a sequence and click Edit Sequence instead of New Sequence.

2. Click New Sequence. The Name Sequence dialog box is displayed.

3. Type a name for the sequence and click OK. The Edit Batch Sequence dialog box is displayed.
4. Click Select Commands.
5. Select a command on the left side of the dialog box and click Add to include it in the list of commands the sequence will run. Repeat for as many commands as you wish the sequence to run.
6. If necessary, select commands on the right side of the dialog box and click Move Up or Move Down to rearrange the order of commands.
7. Click OK. You return to the Edit Batch Sequence dialog box.
8. From the Run Commands On drop-down list, select an option to control which files will be batch processed.
    - Choose Selected Files or Selected Folder and click Browse to choose files or a folder to batch process.
    - Choose Ask When Sequence Is Run to have Acrobat prompt you to select files after you have chosen to run the sequence.
    - Choose Files Open In Acrobat to batch process open files.
9. From the Select Output Location drop-down list, select an output location.
    - Choose Specific Folder and click Browse to designate a folder for the processed file.
    - Choose Ask When Sequence Is Run to have Acrobat prompt you to select an output location after you have chosen to run the sequence.
    - Choose Same Folder As Original(s) to place the processed file in the same location as the original file.
    - Choose Don't Save Changes to have Acrobat process the file and leave it open for editing, not saving it.
10. Click Output Options, specify settings for file naming, output format, and PDF Optimizer if desired.
    - Select File Naming options, such as to add a prefix or suffix to the original file name.
    - Choose whether or not to overwrite older files of the same name with the processed versions.
    - Specify the output format for the processed file.
    - Choose whether or not to enable Fast Web View.
    - Choose whether or not to apply the PDF Optimizer; if so, click Settings to specify its settings.
11. Click OK.

Procedure Reference: Edit a Batch Sequence

To edit batch sequence:

1. Choose Advanced→Batch Processing.
2. In the Batch Sequences dialog box, in the list box, select a batch sequence and click Edit Sequence.
3. The Edit Batch Sequence dialog box is displayed. Click Select Commands.

4. Select a command on the left side of the dialog box and click Add to put it in the list of commands the sequence will run. Repeat for as many commands as you wish the sequence to run.
5. If necessary, select commands on the right side of the dialog box and click Move Up or Move Down to rearrange the order of commands.
6. Click OK to return to the Edit Batch Sequence dialog box.
7. From the Run Commands On drop-down list, select an option to control which files will be batch processed.
   - Choose Selected Files or Selected Folder and click Browse to choose files or a folder to batch process.
   - Choose Ask When Sequence Is Run to have Acrobat prompt you to select files after you've chosen to run the sequence.
   - Choose Files Open In Acrobat to batch process open files.
8. From the Select Output Location drop-down list, select an output location.
   - Choose Specific Folder and click Browse to designate a folder for the processed file.
   - Choose Ask When Sequence Is Run to have Acrobat prompt you to select an output location after you've chosen to run the sequence.
   - Choose Same Folder As Original(s) to place the processed file in the same location as the original file.
   - Choose Don't Save Changes to have Acrobat process the file and leave it open for editing, but not save it.
9. Click Output Options, specify settings for file naming, output format, and PDF Optimizer if desired.
   - Select File Naming options, such as to add a prefix or suffix to the original file name.
   - Choose whether or not to overwrite older files of the same name with the processed versions.
   - Specify the output format for the processed file.
   - Choose whether or not to enable Fast Web View.
   - Choose whether or not to apply the PDF Optimizer; if yes, click Settings to specify its settings.
10. Click OK.

Activity 2-4

Batch Processing Two Advertisements

Activity Time:

10 minutes

Data Files:

- Preliminary Draft Watermark.pdf
- Magazine Ad 2.pdf
- Magazine Ad 3.pdf

1. No documents are open in the Acrobat window.

Scenario:

You frequently need to send out comps (preliminary designs, short for "comprehensive artwork") to circulate for approval, and it's important to you to be able to easily distinguish them from final versions. So, you would like to add a watermark to show that it's a draft document (but only on screen, since the people reviewing it may want to print it to examine it in more detail). Additionally, to make the file transfers to the reviewers as fast as possible, you would like to optimize the files prior to distributing them. You want to avoid doing these steps repeatedly whenever you create a comp, and have an immediate need to process two bike print ad comps you have created.

What You Do	How You Do It
1. **Create a new batch sequence called Add Draft Watermark, and select a command that adds the Preliminary Draft Watermark.pdf file as a watermark at 10% opacity to the document when viewed on screen.**	a. **Choose Advanced→Batch Processing.**
	b. **Click New Sequence.**
	c. In the Choose A Name For This Sequence text box, **type *Add Draft Watermark* and click OK.**
	d. **Click Select Commands.**
	e. **Select Add Watermark & Background and click Add.**

f. **Double-click Add Watermark & Background in the list on the right.**

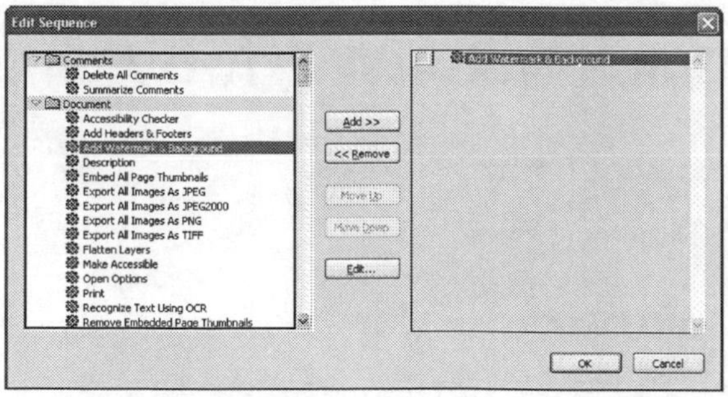

g. **Select the Add A Watermark (Appears On Top Of Page) option.**

h. **Uncheck the Show When Printing check box.**

i. In the Source section, **select the From File option and click Browse.**

j. **Select Preliminary Draft Watermark.pdf and click Open.**

k. **Triple-click in the Opacity text box and type *10***

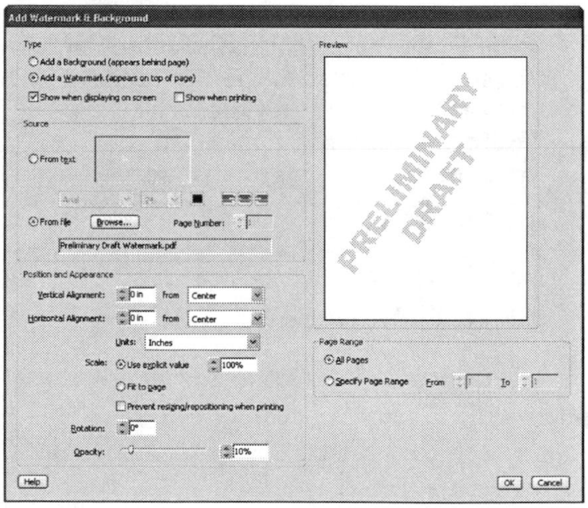

l. **Press Tab.**

m. In the Add Watermark & Background dialog box, **click OK.** In the Edit Batch Sequence - Add Draft Watermark dialog box, **click OK.**

2. **Include the word "Draft" in the file name and run the PDF Optimizer with default settings.**

a. **Verify that Ask When Sequence Is Run is selected from the Run Commands On drop-down list and Same Folder As Original(s) is selected from the Select Output Location drop-down list.**

b. **Click Output Options.**

c. **Select the Add To Original Base Name(s) option.**

d. In the Insert After text box, **type *Draft***

e. **Check the PDF Optimizer check box.**

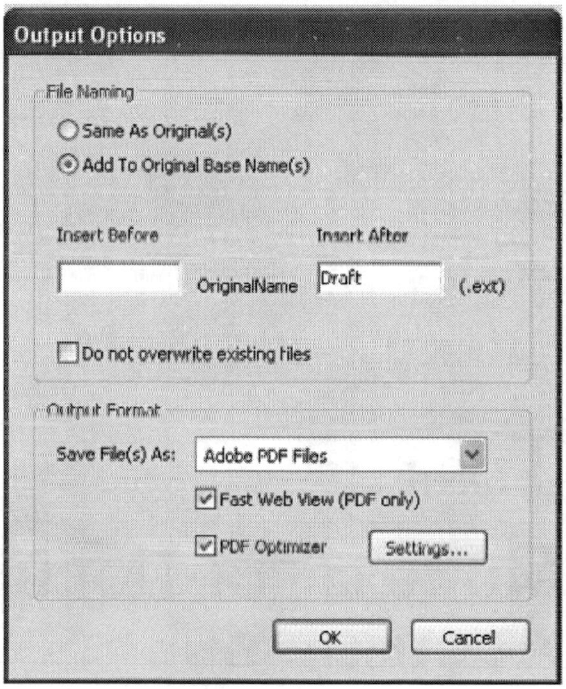

f. In the Output Options dialog box, **click OK.** In the Edit Sequence dialog box, **click OK.**

3. **Run the Add Draft Watermark sequence on the Magazine Ad 2.pdf and Magazine Ad 3.pdf files.**	a. **Verify that the Add Draft Watermark sequence is selected. Click Run Sequence.** b. **Click OK.** c. **Select Magazine Ad 2.pdf and Magazine Ad 3.pdf, then click Select.** d. **Click Close** to close the Batch Sequences dialog box.
4. **Open the files to view their watermarks, then close them when finished.**	a. **Open the Magazine Ad 2Draft.pdf document** to view the watermark. b. **Open the Magazine Ad 3Draft.pdf document** to view the watermark. c. **Close the Magazine Ad 3Draft.pdf document.** d. **Close the Magazine Ad 2Draft.pdf document.**

TOPIC E

Make a PDF Document More Accessible

Making documentation accessible is considered a required business practice. Acrobat provides the tools necessary to check and enhance the accessibility of your PDF documents. In this topic, you will enhance PDF documents so that they are more accessible.

People with visual or mobility impairments commonly use assistive technologies, such as a screen magnifier, to help read on screen content. By making your documents more accessible, you can ensure that everyone can use the content.

Accessibility Options

Accessibility Setup Assistant is a wizard that enables users to change the on-screen appearance of PDFs and how they are handled by a screen reader, screen magnifier, or other assistive technology. Accessibility options available in the Accessibility Setup Assistant dialog box are explained in Table 2-1.

Table 2-1: *Accessibility options*

Accessibility Option	Description
Use High Contrast Colors For Document Text	Allows you to choose from a list of contrasting color combinations for text and background.
Disable Text Smoothing	Makes text sharp and easy to read with a screen magnifier.
Default Display Zoom	Allows you to set a percentage value to magnify documents on the screen. Allows low-vision readers to read reflowed PDF documents more easily.
Always Use The Keyboard Selection Cursor	Keeps the cursor active automatically instead of requiring the user to select the Select tool after a PDF document opens. Select this option if you use a screen magnifier.
Reading Order	Specifies the reading order of untagged documents.
Override The Reading Order In Tagged Document	Uses the reading order specified in the Reading Preferences instead of the one specified by the tag structure of the document. Use this option only when encountering problems in poorly tagged PDF documents.
Confirm Before Adding Tags To Document	When selected, Acrobat will prompt the user to confirm the settings that will be used before it prepares an untagged document for reading by assistive technology.
Deliver Pages Or Document	Deliver Currently Visible Pages option opens one page or a few pages at a time; Deliver The Entire Document At Once option opens the entire document and may negatively affect performance; Deliver All Pages Only For Small Documents option lets Acrobat selectively switch to Page Only mode if the document exceeds the page number limit that you set in Maximum Number Of Pages In A Small Document.
Disable Document Auto-Save	When selected, disables the auto-save function. Each time a PDF document is auto-saved, the screen reader or magnifier must reload the document.
Reopen Documents To The Last Viewed Page	Allows you to save the location you were reading in the document for the next time you open it.
Display PDF Documents In The Web Browser	Opens PDF documents from the Internet in the web browser instead of a separate Acrobat window. Deselect for greater control when navigating a document in a screen reader.

Reading Preferences

The Reading preferences allow you to determine the reading order of the document and how the documents are read by screen readers. You can also set the volume, pitch, and speed, and choose between voices that come with the system.

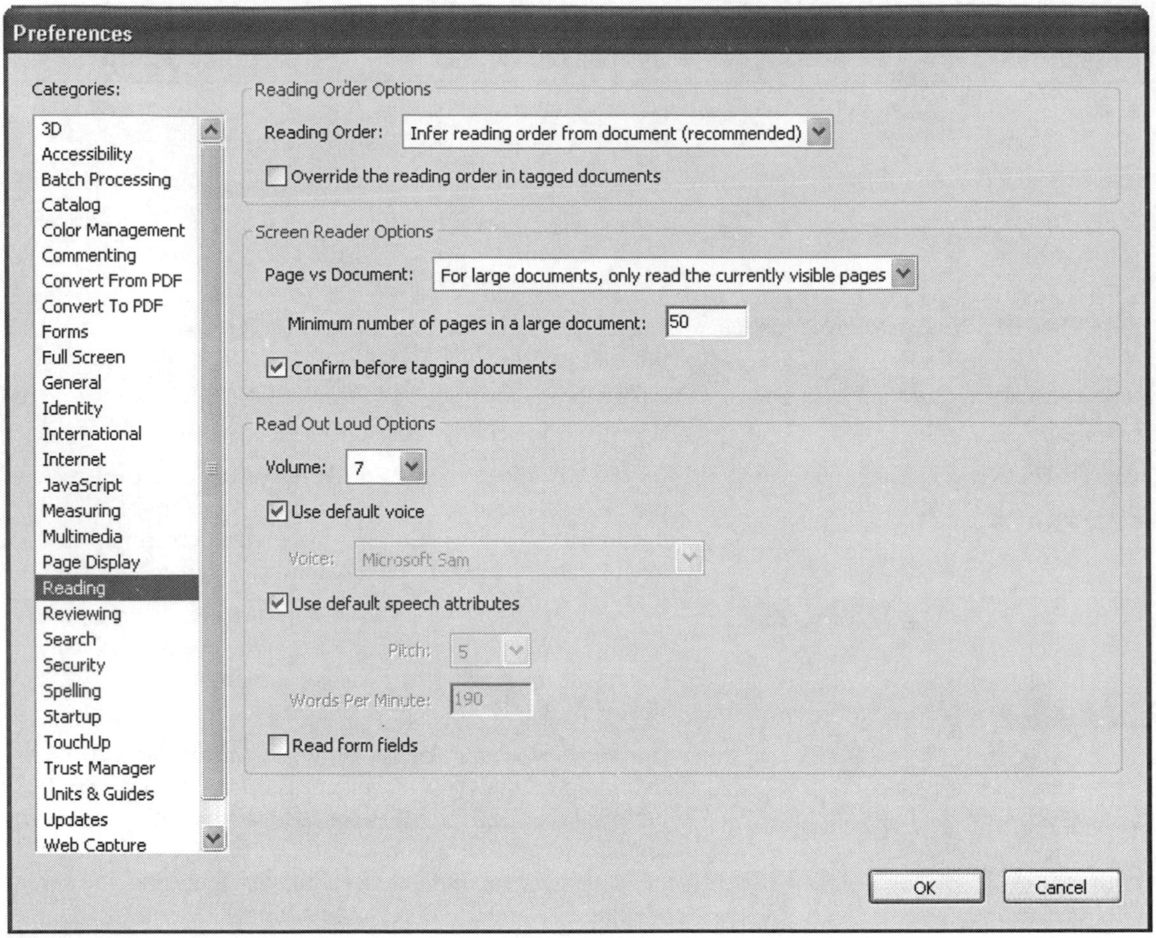

Figure 2-1: *The Reading preferences dialog box*

Tag PDF Documents for Accessibility

A tag is an element that represents a component of a document. A *tagged PDF document* is organized into a logical tree structure containing articles, figures, sections, and subsections. The tags can be rearranged to improve the document reading order. Tags also provide a mechanism for adding alternate text to images so that visually-impaired users can hear a description of the graphic when it's read aloud using screen reader software.

Accessibility Check

Checking PDF documents for accessibility is essential before distributing them to users. The Quick Check command quickly examines the document for structure and tags to determine if it has necessary information to make it accessible to all its users. The Full Check command checks a PDF document for accessibility elements such as alternate text for figures, language for text, character encoding, logical structure tree. A detailed report of the problems encountered during the accessibility check and suggestions for fixing them is displayed.

How to Make a PDF Document More Accessible

Procedure Reference: Add Tags to a Document

To add tags to a document:

1. Open the PDF document.
2. Choose Advanced→Accessibility→Add Tags To Document.

Procedure Reference: View and Edit Existing Tags

If the designer of the tagged document did not complete the tagging process, or if you need to make changes to some of the existing tags, you can make these edits in Acrobat. To edit existing tags:

1. View the Tags navigation pane.
   - Choose View→Navigation Tabs→Tags;
   - Or, click the Tags tab on the navigation pane.

   If you expect that the document will be read aloud using screen reader software, you might also want to check its accessibility by choosing Advanced→Accessibility→Quick Check or Advanced→Accessibility→Full Check.

2. Click the + icon to the left of a tag to expand its contents.

   If you want to access the properties of an object without searching for it in the Tags dialog box, you can select the TouchUp Object tool on the Advanced Editing toolbar and click the object.

3. To determine which document item corresponds to a tag, from the Options menu, choose Highlight Content, then click a tag name. The corresponding item appears in the document pane with a border around it.
4. When you determine the item whose tag you want to edit, click a tag name to select it, and from the Options menu, choose Properties. The TouchUp Properties dialog box is displayed.

   As an example, you might enter an Alternate Text value for a Figure tag to provide text for Screen Reader software to be read aloud instead of the file name.

5. Select the Tag tab, enter property values in the fields, then press Tab to accept the change, and click Close when finished with the dialog box.

Procedure Reference: Check a PDF for Accessibility

To check a PDF for accessibility:

1. Choose Advanced→Accessibility→Full Check.
2. In the Report And Comment Options section, check the Create Accessibility Report check box and click Browse to save a copy of the report to a new location.
3. Check the Create Comments In Document check box to view the report as comments in the PDF document.
4. In the Page Range section, specify the pages you want to include in the accessibility check.

5. In the Checking Options section, specify the options you want to check in the PDF document.
6. Click Start Checking.
7. In the Adobe Acrobat dialog box, click OK. The Accessibility report opens in the How To window with a list of errors and links to where these errors appear in the document.
8. Correct the errors.

Procedure Reference: Setting Accessibility Preferences

To set accessibility preferences using the Accessibility Setup Assistant:

1. Choose Advanced→Accessibility→Setup Assistant.
2. If you use a device that reads text aloud or sends it to a braille output device, select Set Options For Screen Readers.
3. If you use a device that makes text appear larger on screen, select Set Options For Screen Magnifiers.
4. If you use a combination of assistive devices, select Set All Accessibility Options.
5. To use the default settings for accessibility, click Use Recommended Settings And Skip Setup.
6. Work through the steps of the wizard, selecting the appropriate options. If you quit the wizard at any point, Acrobat will use the default setting for accessibility. This is not recommended.
7. Click Done.

Procedure Reference: Reading Order

To view the reading order of page content:

1. Select the TouchUp Reading Order tool.
    - Choose Advanced→Accessibility→TouchUp Reading Order;
    - Or, choose Tools→Advanced Editing→TouchUp Reading Order Tool;
    - Or, on the Advanced Editing toolbar, select the TouchUp Reading Order tool.
2. In the TouchUp Reading Order dialog box, check the Show Page Content Order check box.
3. To show tables and figures, check the Show Tables And Figures check box.
4. Click Close.

ACTIVITY 2-5

Making the Cilantro's Newsletter More Accessible

Activity Time:

5 minutes

Data Files:

- CilantroSnewsAccessible

Scenario:

You have created a CilantroSnewsAccessible.pdf newsletter for the Mexican restaurant Cilantro's. You want the content to be arranged in a hierarchy. You intend to make the newsletter accessible to visually impaired employees also.

What You Do	How You Do It
1. Add tags to the newsletter and view the structure of the document.	a. Choose Advanced→Accessibility→Add Tags To Document.
	b. Choose View→Navigation Tabs→Tags.
	c. Click the + icon to the left of the Tags tag to expand the structure of the document.
	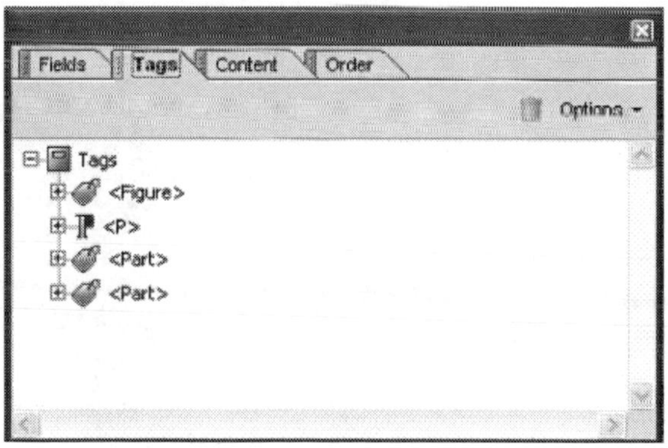
	d. Close the Tags tab.
	e. Save the document.

2. **Check the document for accessibility.**

   a. **Choose Advanced→Accessibility→Full Check.**

   b. In the Report And Comment Options section, **check the Create Accessibility Report check box.**

   c. In the Checking Options section, **verify that the Alternative Descriptions Are Provided check box is checked. Click Start Checking.**

   d. In the Adobe Acrobat dialog box, **click OK.**

   e. In the Accessibility Report, **scroll down to view the Structure Errors section.**

3. **Add the Alternate Text, "Photo of Janet Lignelli" to the second figure on page 1.**

a. **Open the Tags tab.**

b. **Expand the first <Part> tag and then expand the second <P> tag** to locate the second <Figure> tag.

c. **Click the second <Figure> tag.**

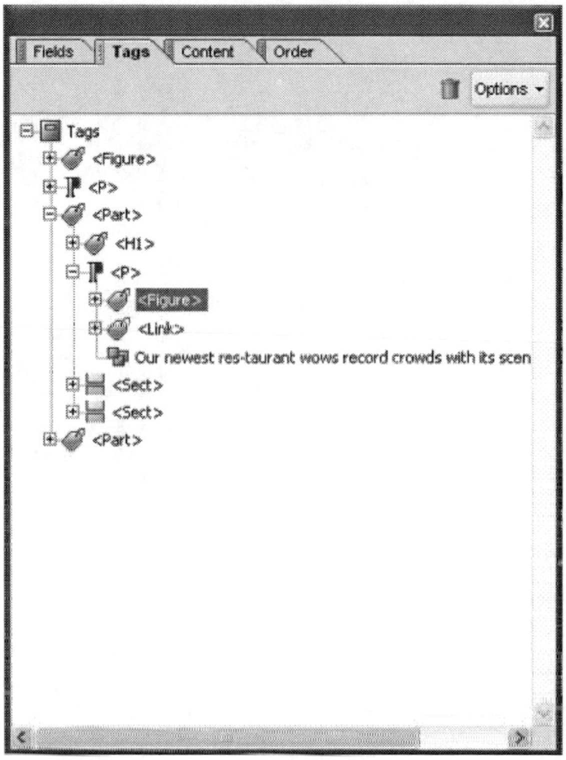

d. From the Options menu, **choose Highlight Content.**

e. From the Options menu, **choose Properties.**

f. In the TouchUp Properties dialog box, **select the Tag tab.**

g. In the Alternate Text text box, **type *Photo of Janet Lignelli***

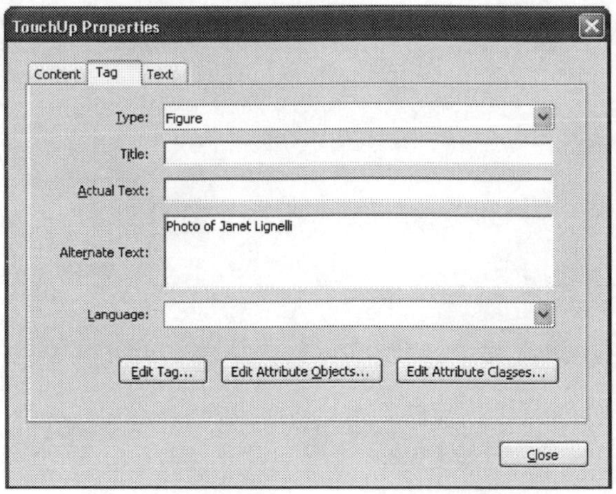

4. **Add the Alternate Text, "Cilantro's at Night" to the third figure on page 1.**

a. **Expand the last <Part> tag and then expand the last <Sect> tag** to locate the third <Figure> tag.

b. **Click the third <Figure> tag.**

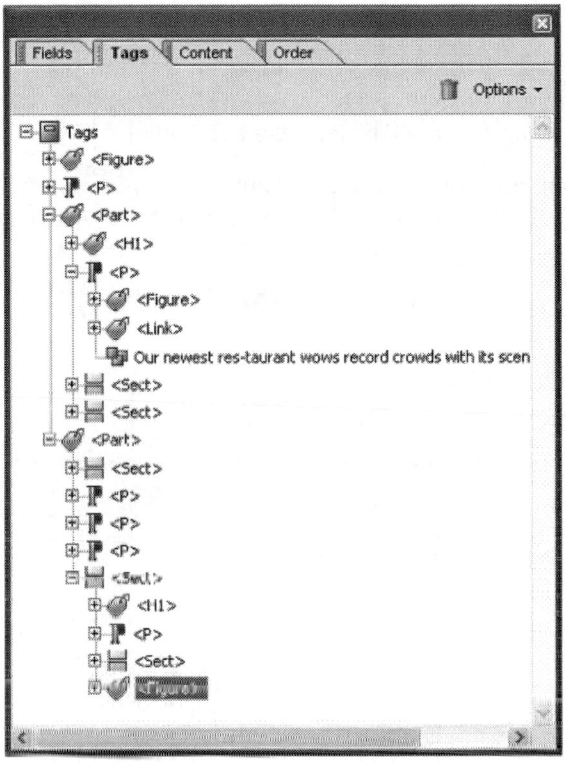

c. In the Alternate Text text box, **type** ***Cilantro's at Night***

d. **Click Close** to close the TouchUp Properties dialog box.

e. **Save the document.**

TOPIC F

Repurpose a PDF Document for Other Displays

One of the ways you can make a PDF document more flexible for reuse is to enhance it so that the PDF can be used on devices other than a computer screen. In this topic, you will repurpose a PDF document for other displays.

In addition to print, existing content is commonly being repurposed for the web, PDAs, and cell phones. Acrobat enables you to reformat existing PDFs for these platforms and devices.

Structured Documents

Definition:

A *structured document* is one that contains a logical structure tree, which defines the intended reading order and hierarchy of information within. The structure tree defines the use of each of its elements, with tags such as Article, Figure, and Story.

Example:

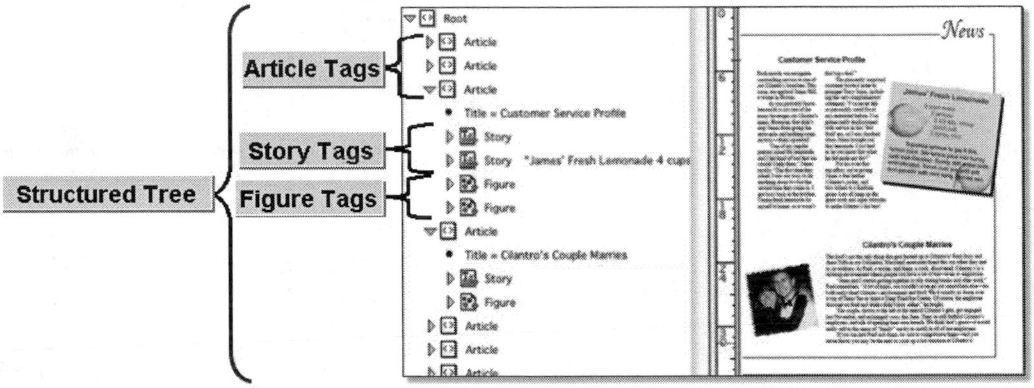

Reflow

Definition:

Reflow is the order in which the elements of a PDF document are displayed on smaller displays without having to scroll horizontally to read each line. In a reflowed document, text remains at its original size even when the window size changes making it easier to view. Reflowed documents cannot be printed or saved. When you reflow a document, articles, paragraphs, tables, images, and formatted lists are reflowed; whereas forms, comments, digital signature fields, page numbers, headers and footers are not.

Example:

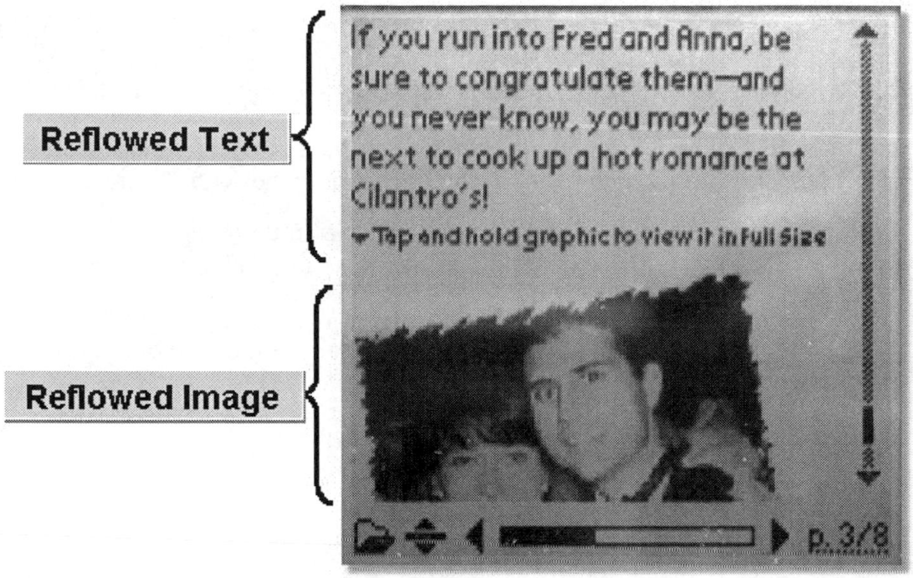

Content Navigation Pane

The Content navigation pane displays a hierarchical view of the objects that make up a PDF document. Each document includes one or more pages and a set of annotations, such as comments and links, and other objects, such as containers, text, paths, and images. You can use the Content navigation pane to correct the reflow problems in a PDF document.

The Content navigation pane provides various options such as, New Container, Edit Container Dictionary, Cut, Paste, Find Content From Selection, Create Artifact, Remove Artifact, Order Selected Content, Highlight Content, and Properties.

How to Repurpose a PDF Document for Other Displays

Procedure Reference: Control Reflow Order for Tagged Adobe PDF Files

To control the reflow order for a tagged PDF file:

1. View the Content navigation pane.
    - Choose View→Navigation Tabs→Content;
    - Or, click the Content tab on the navigation pane if it appears there.
2. Set the magnification at which you want to view the reflowed document.
3. Choose View→Reflow to reflow the document so it appears without requiring horizontal scrolling.
4. Page through the document to examine the order in which the content flows.
5. Return to the original document view.
    - Click either the Actual Size, Fit Page, or Fit Width buttons on the Zoom toolbar;

- Or, choose either the Actual Size, Fit Page, or Fit Width commands in the View menu.

6. In the Content pane, click the + icons to the left of the page you wish to reflow differently to expand its contents.
7. To determine which document item corresponds to a Content pane element, from the Options menu, choose Highlight Content, then click a Content tab element. The corresponding item appears in the document pane with a border around it.
8. Select a range of Content pane elements by selecting one and Shift-clicking another or select multiple non-adjacent elements by clicking one and Ctrl-clicking another.
9. Drag the selected elements above or below others in the Content pane to rearrange them.
10. Reflow the document again to view the new content order.

ACTIVITY 2-6

Control Reflow in the Cilantro's Newsletter

Activity Time:

10 minutes

Data Files:

- CilantroSnewsReusable.pdf

Scenario:

Your coworker has made changes in the newsletter you had created and saved her copy as CilantroSnewsReusable.pdf. She has asked you to check whether the newsletter flows well when viewed on a handheld computer. She also wants you to ensure that the order of text and graphics in each page make sense, and fix any significant problems in the reflow order.

What You Do	How You Do It
1. **Reflow the document to fit the page on the screen and the content in a column, so the viewer won't have to scroll horizontally.**	a. **Choose View→Fit Page.** b. **Choose View→Reflow.**

c. **Press the Page Down key two times** to navigate to the third page.

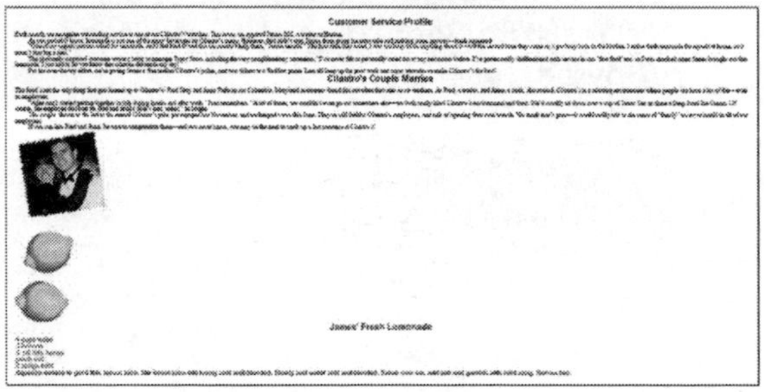

2. **Which page seems to have most content in an illogical order, and what might you do to address the problem?**

3. **Adjust the document's content order so the two lemon graphics and the story about lemonade appear above the Cilantro's Couple Marries story when the document is reflowed.**

a. **Choose View→Fit Page.**

b. **Choose View→Navigation Tabs→ Content.**

c. From the Options menu, **choose Highlight Content.**

d. **Click the + icons to the left of CilantroSnewsReusable.pdf, and to the left of Page 3.**

e. In the Content pane, **scroll down to view the Container <Span> never know, you may be the next to... tag and select the first Path tag after the tag you just located.**

f. **Hold down Shift and click the last Container <Span> tag on page 3.**

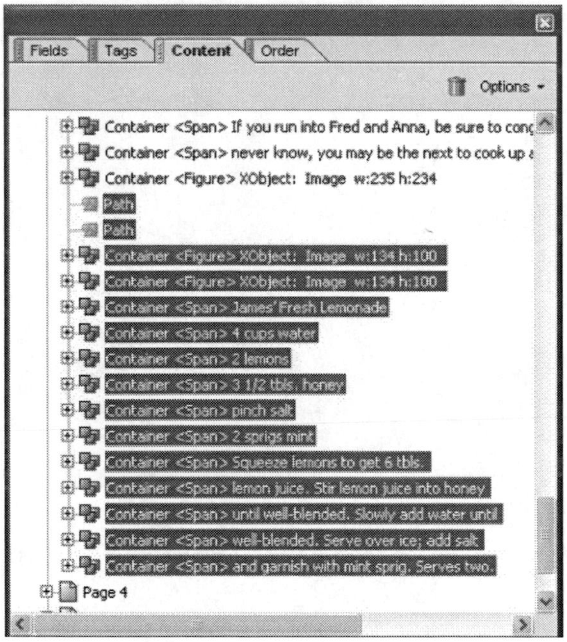

g. **Drag the bottom-right corner handle of the Content pane down. Scroll up to view the selected tags and the Container <Span> to make Cilantro's the best! tag.**

h. **Drag the selected items just below the Container <Span> to make Cilantro's the best! tag.**

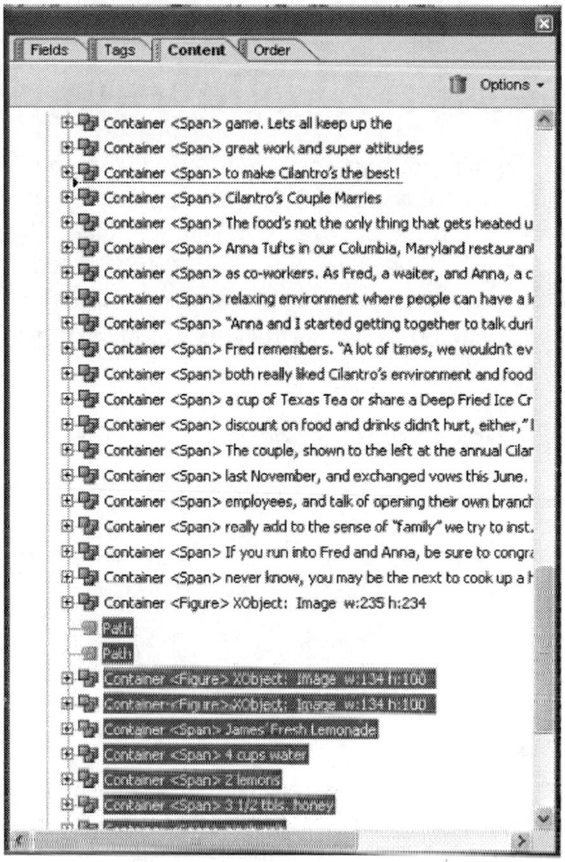

The items may not move the first time you drag, particularly if a "No" mouse pointer appears; make sure a mouse pointer or hand mouse pointer appears along with the triangle that indicates the dragged tags' new location.

i. **Close the Content pane.**

j. **Choose View→Reflow** to view the order of the stories and graphics on page 3.

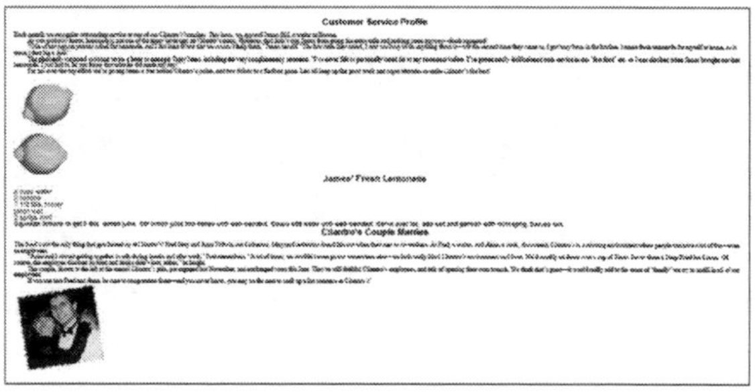

k. **Save and close the document.**

Lesson 2 Follow-up

In this lesson, you enhanced PDF documents by adding multimedia and optimized them for electronic distribution. You also reduced your workload by batch processing documents in preparation for distribution. You also made the information in a PDF document more accessible by adding tags and reflowed the content for other displays. These skills will help you to efficiently enhance your documents and make them available to a wider audience.

1. **How will multimedia make your PDF documents more interesting or communicative?**

2. **Which aspects of designing PDF files for reuse are most important for your documents?**

LESSON 3

Creating Interactive PDF Forms in Adobe Designer

Lesson Time
85 minutes

Lesson Objectives:

In this lesson, you will create interactive PDF forms.

You will:

- Create a new PDF form in Adobe Designer.
- Add text form fields to a PDF form.
- Create fields that can calculate values.
- Create fields with predefined options.
- Create buttons.
- Organize collected data in a spreadsheet.

Introduction

Another way to enhance PDF documents is to create forms that you can distribute, fill out, and submit electronically. In this lesson, you will create interactive PDF forms.

Paper forms can be time-consuming to create, distribute, fill out, and extract information from submitted forms. Adobe Designer enables you to perform these actions quickly and efficiently.

TOPIC A

Create a PDF Form

During the course of a project, you may need to collect information from clients. In this topic, you will begin creating a new form to do this.

Everyday you get dozens of phone calls from people who want to be added to a mailing list. To fulfill a request, you need to get the same details from each person: the person's name, address, and the lists he or she wants to join. In Adobe Designer, you can create forms to help you enter such information consistently.

Adobe Designer

Acrobat 7 Professional includes *Adobe Designer*, which is a client-based, point-and-click tool you can use for creating graphical forms. Designer simplifies XML form creation and enables you to distribute those forms in the PDF or HTML format.

The Designer Window

There are three primary elements of the Designer workspace. The *Layout Editor* is the area where you create the body and master pages for the form design. *Palettes* provide easy access to frequently used tools and include one or more tabs with property information. Four toolbars are installed with Designer: Standard, Font, Paragraph, and Layout.

The Layout Editor includes up to four tabs: Body Pages, Master Pages, XML Source, and PDF Preview. The Body Pages tab is displayed by default. If Acrobat or Reader is installed, the PDF Preview tab is displayed. You can use the View menu to show or hide tabs.

New Form Assistant

The New Form Assistant is a wizard that guides you through a number of steps where you choose the type of form to create, the method of filling it and returning it. Using the New Form Assistant, you can create a new blank form, create a form based on a template, import a PDF document, or import a Word document. The steps in creating a form vary depending on the option you select to create a form in the New Form Assistant dialog box.

PDF Forms

You can use Adobe Designer to create different types of forms.

- **Interactive forms** are forms that a user opens and fills online. Interactive forms can be filled in Acrobat or in Adobe Reader. These forms can include buttons that enable users to save data or send it through email.
- **Static forms** have a fixed layout, regardless of the amount of data entered in the form fields. If more data is entered than the static form was designed to hold, the excess data is not displayed in the form when it is rendered. These forms are simple to create and are filled by Form Server or directly by users in Acrobat or in Adobe Reader.
- **Dynamic forms** have a flowing layout. The layout of the form adjusts itself automatically to the amount of data typed in the form. These forms are filled by Form Server or directly by users in Acrobat or in Adobe Reader. They are useful when you want to present an indeterminate amount of data to users.

Adobe Designer Forms vs. Adobe Acrobat Forms

You can create a form either using Adobe Designer or Adobe Acrobat. The features that Adobe Designer provides for creating forms versus Acrobat forms are listed as follows:

- **Drag and drop objects.** Adobe Designer provides up to twenty three standard form objects that you can drag and drop onto a form. These objects are organized on the Standard tab of the Library palette. You can also use the Custom tab to add custom objects and also create objects and add them to this tab. However, Adobe Acrobat provides seven objects that can be added to the form.
- **Extensive form creation options.** Designer provides you the ability to create a form from scratch or use a template, create an HTML-based form, or explore sample forms. However, Acrobat does not provide the users with such a wide range of options.
- **Form preview.** In Designer, you can preview your form as you design it. The PDF Preview tab will display a PDF form based on your current form design.
- **Interactive barcode form fields.** Designer has the ability to add interactive barcode form fields. The barcode is automatically encoded with the data that users enter in the form. This is a new feature added in Designer which is not available in Acrobat forms.
- **New Form Assistant.** Designer provides a wizard that allows you to open a PDF file and convert it to a fillable form. This wizard also provides steps to select a method how the form will be returned.
- **Integration of a form with its data source.** Designer incorporates Adobe's XDP file format and the ability to integrate and bind forms with databases, web servers, and XML schemas.

When to Use Adobe Designer

In certain situations, creating a form using Acrobat supersedes creating a form using Designer. If you already have a static PDF form that was created in a page-layout application and you need to use some basic form tools to make the form interactive, Acrobat is the tool for you. If you need to create a form from scratch or need to turn a static form into a critical business form by using extensive form tools, use Designer.

Forms: Using Reader versus Using Acrobat

Users can fill an interactive form using Adobe Acrobat Professional, Adobe Acrobat Standard, or Adobe Reader. Using Adobe Acrobat Professional or Adobe Acrobat Standard users can fill the form and save form data; Adobe Reader users can save only a blank copy of the form, unless additional usage rights are added to the form.

Using Adobe Reader you can view, navigate, and print PDF forms, including field data. You can also fill fields within a PDF form. However, Adobe Reader does not support some custom JavaScripts. Therefore, dynamic forms may not function properly when viewed in Adobe Acrobat. However, you can include additional usage rights to the forms to make them function as desired. If a PDF form is right-enabled, you can save forms and form data on your hard disk, fill and submit forms online, distribute forms to others for review and add comments, import and export comments and form data, and also add digital signatures.

Form Creation Process

The steps you perform in Adobe Designer are only a part of the overall process of creating a form. The process of creating a form consists of a number of stages.

1. **Determine the fields.** If you are creating a form from scratch, you should start by determining the fields you will want to use.
2. **Create a rough sketch of the form.** Many designers find it useful to create a rough sketch to determine the basic appearance of the form. This can help you to determine how many pages you will need for your form.
3. **Create the form using Adobe Designer.** Once you have created a basic sketch of your form, you are ready to begin creating the design on screen. Using Designer, you can create a form's design as well as its fields and other elements.
4. **Preview and test the form.** After creating the form you can check how it would appear to the user and test it for functionality.

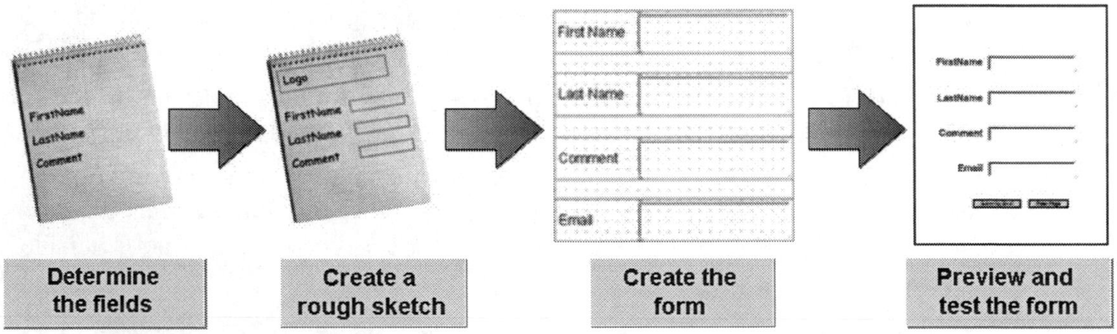

Master and Body Pages

Every form design contains at least one master page that is created by Designer automatically. Master pages facilitate design consistency because they provide a background and layout format for the body pages in a form design. You can use master pages to define the page size and orientation, headers and footers, watermarks and company logos. You can add text, images, and other objects to a master page. You can use the Master pages tab to view, add, delete, and rename master pages.

Body pages represent the pages of a form. Each body page has the same size and orientation as its master page. By default, each body page is associated with the default master page that Designer creates. You can manipulate body pages in the Body Pages tab.

PDF Preview Tab

In the PDF Preview tab, you can view the appearance of your form as you design it. The PDF Preview tab displays a PDF form based on the current form design. You can use the PDF Preview tab to view and test the functionality of the objects you added in your form. The PDF Preview tab appears only when Acrobat or Acrobat Reader is installed.

Form Types

You can save a form in any of the form types as explained in Table 3-1.

Table 3-1: *Form types*

Form Type	Description
Static PDF Form File (*.pdf)	You can use this format to save a form design containing only static elements. If you save a form design containing dynamic elements using this format, the dynamic elements will not be available in the form.
Dynamic PDF Form File (*.pdf)	You can use this format to save the form design containing dynamic elements.
Acrobat 6 Compatible (Static) PDF Form File (*.pdf)	You can use this format to save the form design when you expect the users to fill the form using Acrobat 6.0 or Adobe Reader 6.0.
Adobe XML Form File (*.xdp)	This is Designer's native file format. You can use this format to save the form design in a format that can be interpreted by Form Server.
Adobe Designer Template (*.tds)	You can use this format to save the form design as a template for future use in Designer only. This format provides a starting point for new forms, determining their initial structure and settings.

Form Properties

The Form Properties dialog box displays the properties for the active form. The Form Properties dialog box contains four tabs. The Info tab displays the general information about the form. The Defaults tab allows you to specify standard settings that Designer will use for each form design. The Variables tab allows you to specify form variables. The PDF Security tab allows you to limit the access to the PDF form and restrict certain features such as printing and modifying it.

Info Tab Properties

The properties that you can set using the Info tab are explained in Table 3-2.

Table 3-2: *Info tab properties*

Option	Description
File	Displays the file name and its location.
Title	Displays the name of the form design.
Description	Displays a description of the form design.
Author	Displays the name of the author of the form design.

Option	Description
Contact	Displays additional contact information.
Department	Displays the department of your organization that owns the form design.
Creation Date	Displays the date on which the form design was created.
Version	Displays the current version of the form design.
Version Date	Displays the date of the current version of the form design.

Defaults Tab Properties

The properties that you can set using the Defaults tab are explained in Table 3-3.

Table 3-3: *Defaults tab properties*

Option	Description
Default Locale	Specifies the default language and country for the form design.
Default Language	Specifies the default scripting language to use when authoring a form design. You can select either JavaScript or FormCalc.
Default Run At	Specifies the default location for running the scripts. You can select either of the three options: • **Client** Indicates that the scripts should be run on the client. This is the default option. • **Server** Indicates that the scripts should be run on the server and the result will be sent to the browser. • **Client And Server** Indicates that the scripts can run on both the client and the server.
Preview Type	Specifies the type of the form that you want to preview when using the PDF Preview tab. • **Interactive Form** Select this option to view a form that contains fields for interactive data capture. • **Print Form** Select this option to preview forms that will be printed.
Data File	Specifies the data file to use when previewing how a form design will be merged with data. You can type the path of the data file in the Data File text box or browse to the file.
Allow Form Rendering To Be Cached On Server	When checked, form rendering is cached on the server.

Variables Tab Properties

The properties that you can set using the Variables tab are explained in Table 3-4.

Table 3-4: *Variables tab properties*

Option	Description
Variables	This list box displays all the variables in the current form design.

Option	Description
New button	Click this button to define a new variable. Specify a name for the variable in the Variable list box and it value in the Value list box.
Delete button	Click this button to delete the variable that is selected in the Variable list box.

PDF Security Tab Properties

The properties that you can set using the PDF Security tab are explained in Table 3-5.

Table 3-5: *PDF Security tab properties*

Option	Description
Require A Password To Open The Document	Indicates that the PDF form prompts the user for the password to open the form.
Clear Passwords	Removes the passwords required to open the PDF form, print and edit the document.
Use A Password To Restrict Printing And Editing Of The Document And Its Security Settings	Indicates that the user must provide the correct password in order to print and edit the PDF form.
Printing Allowed	Indicates whether the user can print the form. You can select the printing resolution (Low Resolution (150 dpi) or High Resolution from this drop-down list.
Changes Allowed	Indicates whether the user can make changes to the PDF form. If you allow changes, select the type of change that the user is allowed to make. The options you can select are: Inserting, Deleting, And Rotating Pages, Filling In Form Fields And Signing, Commenting, Filling In Form Fields, And Signing, Any Except Extracting Pages.
Enable Copying Of Text, Images, And Other Content	Indicates that the user can copy text, images, and other content.
Enable Text Access For Screen Reader Devices For The Visually Impaired	Indicates that the user can access the document using a screen reader device.
Enable Plaintext And Metadata	Indicates that the information entered in the Info tab will be saved with the PDF form.

Form Objects

The Library palette contains all the objects that you can add to a form. Table 3-6 provides a list of form objects.

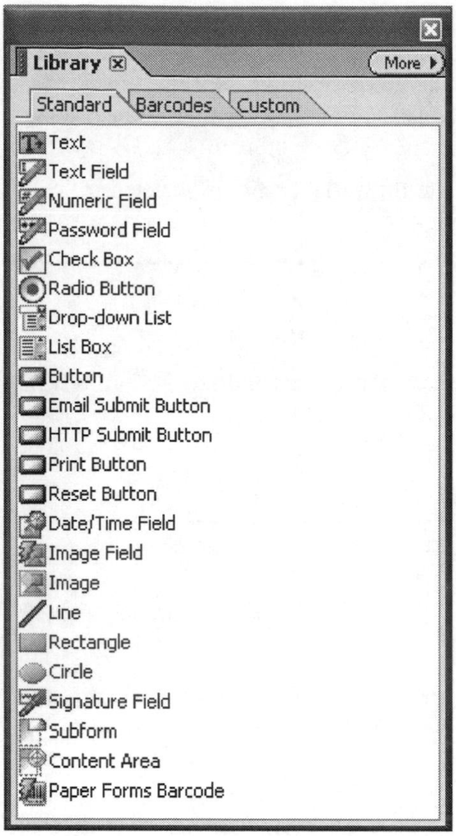

Figure 3-1: *Library palette*

Table 3-6: *Type of form objects*

Object	Description
Text	Text objects present read-only text that form users cannot edit. Text objects can be used to label an area in the form or provide instructions for filling out the form.
Text Field	Text Field accepts and displays textual data. Text Field objects enable users to type, select, edit, cut, copy, paste, and delete any of the text inside the field.
Numeric Field	Numeric Field accepts and displays numeric data. You can use this field to collect or display decimal or integer data.
Password Field	Password Field accepts and masks the display of alphanumeric passwords.
Check Box	Check Box is an object that the user checks or unchecks. Check boxes are often used to display multiple items from which the user may select more than one.
Radio Button	Radio Button is an object that can be used for a relatively small group of items from which the user may select only one. Clicking the radio button next to one item in the group automatically deselects any previously selected radio button in the group.
Drop-down List	Drop-down List is an object that enables the selection of one option from multiple choices. Only one choice is visible until the user opens the list. A drop-down list can be set up to allow the user to manually enter data that may not appear in the list.

Object	Description
List Box	List Box object is similar to a Drop-down List object in that users choose options from a list. However, a list box cannot be set up to allow users to manually enter their own data—they must choose from the existing options in the list. In addition, multiple items in a list box remain visible on screen, and the user can scroll through the list to view additional items. Lastly, you can allow the user to choose more than one item in a list box.
Button	Button is a type of object that the user clicks to cause a particular action to occur. For example, the user may click a button to clear the form fields, or may click a button to submit the form data.
HTTP Submit Button	HTTP Submit Button enables users to return the form data by HTTP post to a specified URL.
Email Submit Button	Email Submit Button enables users to return the form data to a specified email address.
Print Button	Print Button is configured to enable users to print the form.
Reset Button	Reset Button can be clicked to reset the contents of the form's fields to their default values.
Date/Time Field	Date/Time Field accepts and displays data about the date, the time, or both.
Image Field	Image Field is a placeholder for loading an image dynamically when the form is rendered.
Image	Image is an object that displays images such as company logos or icons.

Other Form Objects

Object	Description
Line	Line is an object that can be used to draw solid, dashed, or dotted lines on a form.
Circle	Circle is an object that can be used to draw circular, elliptical, or arc shapes on a form.
Rectangle	Rectangle is an object that can be used to draw rectangles with regular, notched, or rounded corners.
Signature Field	Signature Field is an object that enables users to attach an electronic signature to the form.
Subform	Subform is a container that controls the positioning of objects. A subform can contain non-interactive objects, such as lines, circles, rectangles, text, and images.
Content Area	Container Area is a container that serves as the top-level object in an object hierarchy.
Paper Forms Barcode	Paper Forms Barcode is a 2D barcode that encodes the data entered by users in an interactive form.

Library Palette

The Library palette contains all the objects that you can add to a form. The objects are organized into three groups and placed on the tabs, namely Standard, Barcodes, and Custom. The Standard tab contains the core drawing objects that can be added to a form. The Custom tab contains the custom objects included in Designer. You can create custom objects and add them to the Custom tab. Creating custom objects saves you a lot of time because you don't have to create the objects and all their properties. The Barcodes tab contains a list of standard barcode objects. Barcodes are usually used to identify forms. You can also create a paper form barcode. This barcode electronically captures the information entered by the respondent in a form.

Object Properties

You can change the properties of the objects added to a form. You can change an object's layout, border, font, paragraph, and accessibility properties as explained in Table 3-7.

Table 3-7: *Object properties*

Properties	Options and Description
Layout	• **X and Y text boxes** Set the horizontal and vertical position of the object's anchor points. • **Width, Height, and Expand to Fit/ Auto-Fit** Sets the minimum height and width of the object and enables expansion in that direction. The Auto-Fit option appears for text and subform objects only. When selected the object changes size to fit the enclosed content. • **Anchor** Sets the object's anchor point. • **Rotation** Rotates the object around its anchor point. • **Margins** Sets the amount of white space on the left and right sides of the object and above and below the object. • **Caption** Sets the position of the caption. • **Reserve** Sets the amount of space reserved for a caption.
Border	• **Edges** Sets the border properties for all or individual edges. • **Style options** Sets the style and width for the borders. • **Line Color** Sets the line color. • **Corners** Applies a style to border corners. • **Radius** Sets the radius of notched corners. • **Background Style** Sets the background fill style or pattern. • **Background Fill Color** Sets the background fill colors.
Font	• **Font** Sets the typeface. • **Size** Sets the typeface size. • **Base Shift** Sets the offset of the characters relative to the baseline. • **Style** Sets the typeface style.

Properties	Options and Description
Paragraph	• **Horizontal Alignment options** The Align Left option left-aligns the caption or value. The Align Center option center-aligns and the Align Right option right-aligns the caption or value. The Justify option justifies the caption or value. • **Numeric Alignment option** Sets the alignment options for numeric fields based on the radix. • **Vertical Alignment options** The Align Top option aligns to the top of the area reserved for the caption or value. The Align Bottom option aligns to the bottom of the area reserved for the caption or value. • **Indents** Sets the left and right indents. • **First** Sets the first line indent. The None option indents all the lines by the same amount. The First Line option indents the first line only. The Hanging option indents all the lines except the first. • **By** Sets the amount of the first line or hanging indent. • **Spacing** Sets the amount of vertical space above and below the paragraph. • **Line Spacing** Sets the amount of space between lines.
Accessibility	• **Tooltip** Sets a tooltip for the object. • **Screen Reader Precedence** Indicates which setting the screen reader should read first. The options available are Custom Text, Tooltip, Caption, Name, and None. • **Custom Screen Reader Text** Sets a custom text for the selected object. The screen reader reads the text entered in this box.

Form Layout Options

You can align, distribute, center, group, ungroup, and merge the objects in a form using the commands (Table 3-8) available in the Layout menu.

Table 3-8: *The Form Layout options*

Command	Description
Align→Left	Aligns the left edges of the selected objects to match the position of the object in the selection that was selected last.
Align→Right	Aligns the right edges of the selected objects to match the position of the object in the selection that was selected last.
Align→Top	Aligns the top edges of the selected objects to match the position of the object in the selection that was selected last.
Align→Bottom	Aligns the bottom edges of the selected objects to match the position of the object in the selection that was selected last.
Align→Vertical Center	Aligns the vertical midpoint of the selected objects.

Command	Description
Align→Horizontal Center	Aligns the horizontal midpoint of the selected objects.
Align→To Grid	Aligns the selected objects to the closest grid point.
Distribute→Across	Evenly distributes the selected objects horizontally.
Distribute→Down	Evenly distributes the selected objects vertically.
Distribute→In Rows & Columns	Aligns and evenly distributes the selected objects in rows and columns.
Center In Page→Horizontally	Centers the selected objects horizontally on the form design.
Center In Page→Vertically	Centers the selected objects vertically on the form design.
Make Same Size→Width	Changes the size of the selected objects to match the width of the object in the selection that was selected last.
Make Same Size→Height	Changes the size of the selected objects to match the height of the object in the selection that was selected last.
Make Same Size→Both	Changes the size of the selected objects to match the height and width of the object in the selection that was selected last.
Group	Combines the selected objects so that they function as a single unit.
Ungroup	Breaks a group object into separate units.
Merge Selected Text Objects	Merges the contents of multiple text objects into a single object.
Wrap In A New Radio Button Group	Wraps the selected radio button objects into a single object.
Merge Radio Button Group	Merges the selected radio button group(s) into a single radio button group.
Bring To Front	Moves the selected objects to the foreground.
Bring Forward	Moves the selected objects forward relative to other objects that are in front of them.
Send Backward	Moves the selected objects backward relative to other objects that are behind them.
Send To Back	Moves the selected objects to the background.

Other Form Layout Options

How to Create a PDF Form

Procedure Reference: Create a New Form

To create a new form:

1. Choose Start→All Programs→Adobe Designer 7.0.
2. Click Close to dismiss the Welcome Screen.
3. Choose File→New.
4. In the New Form Assistant dialog box, on the Getting Started page, click Next.

5. On the Setup: New Blank Form page, click Next, to accept the default form settings.
6. On the Return Method page, click Next, to accept the default method to distribute and collect the form.
7. On the Return Information: Submit By Email page, in the Return Email Address text box, enter the email addresses of the form recipients and click Finish.
8. If necessary, select the Submit By Email button by clicking on it and reposition it as needed.
9. Choose File→Save As.
10. In the File Name text box, type a name.
11. Click Save.

Procedure Reference: Add Text to the Form

To add text object to the form:

1. From the Library palette, select the Text object and place it on the Layout Editor:
   - Drag the object from the Library palette onto the Layout Editor;
   - Or, double-click the object on the Library palette;
   - Or, click and drag on the Layout Editor.
2. Select the default text on the text object and type the new text.
3. Select the text, and on the Font toolbar, from the Font Style drop-down list, select the appropriate style.
4. On the Font toolbar, from the Font Size drop-down list, select the appropriate size.
5. On the Paragraph toolbar, click the appropriate button to change the text alignment.
6. If necessary, choose Layout→Center In Page→Horizontally to center the Text object horizontally.
7. Choose File→Save to save the changes made to the form.

Procedure Reference: Add Image to the Form

To add image object to the form:

1. On the Library palette, double-click the Image object.
2. On the Layout Editor, double-click the image object to display the Browse For Image File dialog box.
3. Navigate to the image that you want to insert and click Open.
4. Select the image and reposition it as needed.
5. Choose File→Save to save the changes made to the form.

Procedure Reference: Resize Objects

To resize an object:

1. Select the object that is to be resized.

2. Position the mouse pointer over one of the selection handles so that it turns into a double-headed arrow.
3. Resize the object:
   - To make the object smaller, click and drag the selection handle toward the middle of the object.
   - To make the object bigger, click and drag the selection handle away from the object.

Procedure Reference: Add Body Page

To add a body page to the form:

1. If required, select the Body Pages tab.
2. Choose Insert→New Body Page to add a new body page to the form.
3. If necessary, choose Insert→Delete Body Page to delete the body page.

Procedure Reference: Add Master Page

To add a master page to the form:

1. Display the Master Pages tab:
   - Choose View→Master Pages;
   - Or, select the Master Pages tab.
2. Choose Insert→New Master Page.
3. If necessary, choose Insert→Delete Master Page to delete the master page.

Procedure Reference: Set the Properties of a Form Object

To set the properties of the Email Submit Button object:

1. Click on the Email Submit Button object on the Layout Editor to select it.
2. From the Appearance drop-down list, select the appropriate border style.
   - No Border: Removes the line around the button.
   - Solid Border: Create a thick line around the button.
   - Raised Border: Creates a shadow around the button and gives a three-dimensional effect to it.
   - Custom: Displays the Custom Appearance dialog box that can be used to give a customized look to the button.
3. If required, in the Email Address text box, type the email address to which the form data is to be sent.
4. In the Email Subject text box, type the subject of the email message.
5. From the Presence drop-down list, select the appropriate option.
   - Visible: The button is visible and occupies some space on the body page in the form.
   - Invisible: The button is invisible, but still occupies some space on the body page in the form.
   - Hidden (Exclude From Layout) : The button is invisible and does not occupy space on the form.

- Visible (But Don't Print) : The button is visible on the form but is not displayed on the printed output.
- Invisible (But Print Anyway) : The button is not visible on the form but is displayed on the printed output.

6. From the Locale drop-down list, select the appropriate option to specify a locale for language.
    - Default Locale: Presents data according to the Default Locale settings specified in the Defaults tab of the Form Properties dialog box.
    - Viewer's System Locale: Presents data as per the locale settings of the user's computer.
7. Choose File→Save to save the changes made to the form.

Selecting Objects

You can select any object on the form by clicking it. To select multiple objects, you can either hold down Ctrl and click each of them or click and drag the pointer over them. If you need to select all objects on the form, you can use the Select All option in the Edit menu.

Procedure Reference: Create a Toolbar

To create a toolbar:

1. Choose Tools→Customize Toolbars.
2. In the Toolbars tab, click New.
3. In the Toolbar Name text box, type a name for the toolbar and click OK.
4. Select the Command tab.
5. In the Categories list box, select the required Category.
6. In the Buttons section, select the button that you want to add to the toolbar.
7. Repeat steps 5 and 6 to add as many buttons as required to the toolbar.
8. If required, drag a button off the toolbar to delete the button.
9. Click OK.
10. If required, click and drag the toolbar to the top of the Designer window to dock it.
11. If required, click and drag the toolbar to move it to a new location.

Procedure Reference: Show a Toolbar

To show a toolbar:

1. Right-click a toolbar.
2. Select the toolbar that you want to show.

Procedure Reference: Hide a Toolbar

To hide a toolbar:

1. Right-click a toolbar.
2. Deselect the toolbar that you want to hide.

Procedure Reference: Delete a Toolbar

To delete a toolbar:

1. Choose Tools→Customize Toolbars.
2. In the Toolbars tab, in the Toolbars list box, select the toolbar that you want to delete.

   You can delete only those toolbars that you have created.

3. Click Delete.
4. Click OK.

Procedure Reference: Reset a Toolbar

To reset a toolbar:

1. Choose Tools→Customize Toolbars.
2. In the Toolbars tab, in the Toolbars list box, select the Toolbar that you want to reset.
3. Click Reset.
4. Click OK.

Procedure Reference: Manage Palettes

To manage palettes:

1. If necessary, move the palette to the required position:
   - Hold down Control and drag the palette to the required position.
   - Drag the palette tab to the destination palette window and release it to move target palette into the destination palette window.
2. If necessary, dock the palettes:
   - Drag the palette bar to the bottom of another palette and release it to dock the palettes together.
   - Drag the palette bar to the side of the Adobe Designer window to dock it beside the window.
3. Position the mouse pointer on any side or corner of the palette so that the double-headed arrow is displayed, and then click and drag to resize the palette, as needed.

ACTIVITY 3-1

Creating a PDF Form

Activity Time:

10 minutes

Scenario:

The marketing department at Super Fast Wheels decided that the company's mailing list could be enlarged significantly by collecting prospective customer names and personal information through an online promotion. With input from them, you are planning to create a PDF form with the overall design and the questions in place.

What You Do	How You Do It
1. **Display the New Form Assistant dialog box in Adobe Designer.**	a. **Choose Start→All Programs→Adobe Designer 7.0.**
	b. **Click Close** to dismiss the Welcome Screen.
	c. **Choose File→New** to display the New Form Assistant dialog box.
2. **Using the New Form Assistant dialog box, create a new form using all the default settings and james@example.com as the email address.**	a. In the New Form Assistant dialog box, on the Getting Started page, **click Next.** Using the New Form Assistant, you can create a form from scratch, based on a template, or by importing a PDF or Word document.
	b. On the Setup: New Blank Form page, **click Next,** to accept the default form settings.
	c. On the Return Method page, **click Next,** to accept the default Fill Then Submit method.
	d. On the Return Information: Fill Then Submit page, in the Return Email Address text box, **type** ***james@example.com***
	e. **Click Finish.**

3. **Based on the default settings in the New Form Assistant, which button is automatically added to the new form?**

   a) HTTP Submit button

   b) Submit By Email button

   c) Print button

   d) Reset button

4. **Create a body page and position the Submit By Email button at the bottom-center of the second page.**	a. **Choose Insert→New Body Page.** b. **Choose Edit→Cut.** c. **Scroll down and click in the second page of the form.** d. **Choose Edit→Paste.** e. **Click and drag the Submit By Email button to the bottom of the Layout Editor.** f. **Choose Layout→Center In Page→Horizontally.**
5. **Add a text object to the first page of the form and replace the default text with the words Register for a Chance to Win a Motorcycle.**	a. **Scroll up and click in the first page of the form.** b. In the Library palette, **double-click the Text object.** c. On the Layout Editor, **click and drag the text object to the 6-inch mark on the vertical ruler and the 4.5-inch mark on the horizontal ruler.** d. **Position the mouse pointer on the bottom-right selection handle of the text object, and click and drag to the 7.5-inch mark on the vertical ruler and the 8-inch mark on the horizontal ruler.** e. **Click OK** to dismiss the message box displayed. f. **Double-click in the text object** to select the default text. g. **Type *Register for a Chance to Win a Motorcycle***

6. **Format the font of the text object and set it to Freestyle Script with size 36.**	a. **Position the mouse pointer inside the text object and click three times** to select the words Register for a Chance to Win a Motorcycle. b. On the Font toolbar, **click the Font Style drop-down arrow.** c. **Scroll up the Font Style drop-down list and select Freestyle Script.** d. On the Font toolbar, from the Font Size drop-down list, **select 36.** e. On the Paragraph toolbar, **click the Center Align button** to center the text.
7. **Add the motorcycle.jpeg file to the left of the Layout Editor.**	a. **Scroll up to view the top of the page.** b. On the Library palette, **scroll down to view the Image object.** c. **Click the Image object.** d. On the Layout Editor, **click at the intersection of the 1-inch mark on the vertical and horizontal ruler.** e. On the Layout Editor, **double-click the Image object** to display the Browse For Image File dialog box. f. **Click My Computer.** g. **Navigate to the C:\084173Data\Interactive PDF\Activity1\Start folder.** h. **Select the motorcycle.jpeg file and click Open.** i. **Place the mouse pointer on the bottom-right selection handle, and click and drag downward and to the right to the 5.5-inch mark on the vertical ruler and the 8-inch mark on the horizontal ruler.**

8.	**Add the superfastlogo.jpeg file to the top-left corner on the second page of the form.**	a. **Scroll down and click in the second page of the form.** b. On the Library palette, **double-click the Image object.** c. On the Layout Editor, **click and drag the image object to align its top-left edge to the 0.5-inch mark on the vertical and the horizontal ruler.** d. On the Layout Editor, **double-click the image object** to display the Browse For Image File dialog box. e. **Select the superfastlogo.jpeg file and click Open.** f. **Position the mouse pointer in the right-center boundary of the image object, and click and drag the selection handle to the right till the 8-inch mark on the horizontal ruler.**
9.	**Save the form as Spring05PromotionForm.pdf.**	a. **Choose File→Save As.** b. **Click My Computer.** c. **Navigate to the C:\084173Data\Interactive PDF\Activity1\Solution folder.** d. In the File Name text box, **type** ***Spring05PromotionForm.pdf*** e. **Click Save.** f. **Choose File→Close.** g. **Click Close** to dismiss the Welcome Screen.

TOPIC B

Add Text Form Fields

Almost every form includes fields in which the respondent can type data. In this topic, you will create and label text fields.

Text fields are the most open-ended of the field types, because they allow any kind of response.

How to Add Text Form Fields

Procedure Reference: Add Text Field Object to a Form

To add a text field object to a form:

1. On the Standard tab of the Library palette, double-click the Text Field object.
2. Select the default caption text and type a new caption.
3. On the Object palette, in the Field tab, check Allow Multiple Lines to enable multiple lines of text.
4. Check Limit Length and specify the maximum number of characters in the Max Chars text box.
5. Position the mouse pointer in the boundary line between the Field Caption and Field Value so that the double-headed arrow is displayed and click and drag the boundary line in the required direction to resize the space between them.
6. On the Object palette, select the Binding tab and, in the Name text box, select the default text and type a new name for the object.

Procedure Reference: Duplicate Objects

To create a single duplicate of a field:

1. Select the object.
2. Duplicate the object:
   - Choose Edit→Copy, then Edit→Paste;
   - Or, choose Edit→Duplicate.

Procedure Reference: Group Objects

To group objects in the form:

1. Select the objects:
   - Ctrl-click the objects that you want to group on the Layout Editor;
   - Or, choose Window→Hierarchy to display the Hierarchy palette and Ctrl-click the objects that you want to group in the Hierarchy palette.
2. Group the objects:
   - Choose Layout→Group;
   - Or, on the Layout toolbar, click the Group Objects button.

Procedure Reference: Ungroup Objects

To ungroup objects in the form:

1. Select the group either on the Layout Editor or the Hierarchy palette.
2. Ungroup objects:
   - Choose Layout→Ungroup;
   - Or, on the Layout toolbar, click the Ungroup Objects button.

Procedure Reference: Add Objects to a Group Using the Layout Editor

To add objects to a group using the Layout Editor:

1. Select the object on the Layout Editor.
2. Drag the object to the group that you want to add it to.

Procedure Reference: Add Objects to a Group Using the Hierarchy Palette

To add objects to a group using the Hierarchy palette:

1. Choose Window→Hierarchy to display the Hierarchy palette.
2. Select the object in the Hierarchy palette.
3. Drag the object to the node of the group that you want to add the object to.

Procedure Reference: Lock Objects

To lock objects:

1. Choose Edit→Lock Static Objects to lock all static objects.
2. Choose Edit→Lock Fields to lock all field objects.

   Objects that are locked cannot be selected or edited.

3. If required, choose Edit→Lock Text to lock all text in the form objects.

Procedure Reference: Resizing Objects to the Same Size

To resize objects to the same size:

1. Ctrl-click the objects that are to be made the same size.
2. Choose Layout→Make Same Size.
3. In the submenu displayed, choose the appropriate dimension.
   - Width: To change the width of the selected objects to match the width of the last object selected.
   - Height: To change the height of the selected objects to match the height of the last object selected.
   - Both: To change both the width and height of the selected objects to match the width and height of the last object selected.

Procedure Reference: Change the Properties of Multiple Objects

To change the properties of multiple objects:

1. Ctrl-click the objects whose properties are to be changed.

2. Right-click and choose the appropriate property to be modified and perform the modifications.

Depending upon the objects selected the properties available for modification will vary.

Procedure Reference: Delete an Object

To delete an object on the form:

1. Select the object.
2. Choose Edit→Delete.

Procedure Reference: Copy and Paste Objects

To copy and paste objects:

1. Ctrl-click the objects to be copied.
2. Choose Edit→Copy.
3. Choose Edit→Paste.
4. Reposition the objects as needed.

Naming Objects

You can name objects using the conventions agreed upon by you and people you work with. For example, you might begin each object name with an abbreviation that indicates the field type. You can use a naming convention to help those working on the form to identify an object looking at its name. For example, you could use the following abbreviations to name objects:

Object Type	Abbreviation
Button	bt
Check Box	ch
Drop-down List	dl
List Box	lb
Radio Button	rb
Text	tx
Text Field	tf
Signature	sg

For example, a text field that is used to obtain a respondent's name could be named tfName using this convention. When creating your own forms, you can name fields with or without abbreviations such as these.

ACTIVITY 3-2

Creating Text Field Objects

Activity Time:

10 minutes

Data Files:

- Spring05PromotionForm.pdf

Scenario:

You now need to create the interactive part of the Spring05PromotionForm.pdf to allow the respondent to type information on the page. You also want the text field formatting to match the text formatting, Arial, 12 point.

What You Do	How You Do It
1. **Create a text field object named tfFirst.**	a. **Choose File→Open** to display the Open dialog box.
	b. **Click My Computer.**
	c. **Navigate to the C:\084173Data\Interactive PDF\Activity2\Start folder.**
	d. **Select the Spring05PromotionForm.pdf file and click Open.**
	e. **Scroll down and click in the second page of the form.**
	f. On the Library palette, **click the Text Field object.**
	g. On the Layout Editor, **click at the intersection of the 2.5-inch mark on the vertical ruler and the 3-inch mark on the horizontal ruler.**
	h. On the Object palette, **select the Binding tab.**
	i. **Double-click in the Name text box and type *tfFirst***

2.	**Format the caption of the tfFirst object so that the Font Type is set to Arial and the Font Size is set to 12. Change the caption on the tfFirst object to First Name and make it an entry that must be filled in by the user.**	a. **Choose Edit→Lock Text.** b. **Position the mouse pointer on the bottom right selection handle of the tfFirst object to display the double-headed arrow.** c. **Click and drag to the 3-inch mark on the vertical ruler and the 6-inch mark on the horizontal ruler.** d. **Double-click in the caption part of the tfFirst object.** e. In the Font toolbar, **click the Font Style drop-down arrow.** f. **Scroll up and select Arial.** g. In the Font toolbar, from the Font Size drop-down list, **select 12.** h. **Type *First Name*** i. On the Object palette, **select the Value tab.** j. From the Type drop-down list, **select User Entered - Required.**
3.	**Duplicate the tfFirst object and position the duplicate beneath the tfFirst object. Then, rename the duplicate object as tfLast and change the caption for the tfLast object to Last Name.**	a. **Choose Edit→Duplicate.** b. **Click and drag the duplicate object to align its top-left edge to the 3.5-inch mark on the vertical ruler and the 3-inch mark on the horizontal ruler.** c. On the Object palette, **select the Binding tab.** d. **Double-click in the Name text box and type *tfLast*** e. On the Layout Editor, **double-click in the caption part of the tfLast object and type *Last Name***

4. **Group the tfFirst and the tfLast objects.**	a. **Select the tfFirst object.** b. **Hold down Ctrl and click the tfLast object.** c. **Choose Layout→Group.**
5. **Create a text field object, position it beneath the tfLast object, and name it as tfComment.**	a. On the Library palette, **click the Text Field object.** b. On the Layout Editor, **click at the intersection of the 4.5-inch mark on the vertical ruler and the 3-inch mark on the horizontal ruler.** c. On the Object palette, on the Binding tab, **double-click in the Name text box and type *tfComment***
6. **Change the caption for the tfComment object to Comment and resize it to match that of the tfLast object.**	a. **Double-click in the caption part of the tfComment object and type *Comment*** b. **Ctrl-click the tfLast object.** c. **Choose Layout→Make Same Size→Both.** d. **Click in a blank area of the Layout Editor** to deselect the selected objects. e. **Format the font of the tfComment object and set it to Arial, 12.**
7. **Using the tfComment object, create another text field. Name this duplicate object as tfEmail and position it directly beneath the tfComment object.**	a. **Choose Edit→Duplicate.** b. **Click and drag the duplicate object to align its top-left edge to the 5.5-inch mark on the vertical ruler and the 3-inch mark on the horizontal ruler.** c. **Double-click in the caption part of the duplicate object and type *Email*** d. On the Object palette, on the Binding tab, **double-click in the Name text box and type *tfEmail***

8.	**Add the tfComment and tfEmail objects to the existing Group.**	a. **Choose Window→Hierarchy** to display the Hierarchy palette. b. In the Hierarchy palette, **click and drag the tfComment object to the Group node.** c. In the Hierarchy palette, **click and drag the tfEmail object to the Group node.** d. **Close the Hierarchy palette.**
9.	**Lock the objects on the form and save the file.**	a. **Choose Edit→Lock Fields.** b. **Choose Edit→Lock Static Objects.** c. **Choose File→Save As.** d. **Click the Up One Level button.** e. **Double-click the Solution folder.** f. **Click Save.** g. **Close the file.** h. **Click Close** to dismiss the Welcome Screen.

TOPIC C

Create Calculations

Many forms need places for the respondent to enter numeric data. In this topic, you will create fields capable of performing calculations.

Calculations can perform mathematical functions automatically, so the user is not required to perform any calculations of his or her own.

How to Create Calculations

Procedure Reference: Calculate Values

To calculate values:

1. Choose Window→Script Editor.
2. In the Script Editor, position the mouse pointer above the Show drop-down list and double-click to display the multiline version of the Script Editor.
3. Reposition the Script Editor as needed.
4. On the Layout Editor, select the object by which the calculation event is to be triggered.
5. In the Script Editor, from the Show drop-down list, select the event that is to trigger the function or script. Events with calculations or script attached to them are displayed with an asterix (*) next to the Event name.

   Events that are not applicable to a particular object appear dimmed out.

6. From the Language drop-down list, select the language that you want to use:
   - FormCalc: Native Adobe calculation language that can be used for small and simple scripts.
   - JavaScript: Powerful and flexible scripting language that can be used for complex scripts.
7. From the Run At drop-down list, select where the function or script is to execute:
   - Client: Executes the function or script when the client application processes the form.
   - Server: Executes the function or script when the server application processes the form.
   - Client and Server: Executes the function or script when either the client or the server processes the form.
8. Specify either the calculation or script that is to be executed:
   - Click the Function button, and from the drop-down list that is displayed, select the appropriate built-in function for the calculation to be performed, press Enter, and in the Script Source Field make changes specific to the calculation to be performed.

- Click in the Script Source Field and type the script for the calculation that is to be performed.

9. Click the Enter Script Source Changes button to save the changes made.
10. If required, click the Cancel Script Source Changes to undo the changes made.
11. Click the Enter Script Source Changes button to add the calculation to the form.

Procedure Reference: Adjust Tab Order

To set the tab order:

1. Choose View→Tab Order.
2. Click OK to dismiss the Tab Order message box.
3. Select the object that you want to be the first in the tabbing order.
4. Select each of the remaining objects in the order in which they are to be accessed.
5. Choose View→Tab Order to dismiss the tabbing order number displayed on the objects.

Procedure Reference: Test a PDF Form

To test a PDF form:

1. Choose File→Form Properties.
2. Select the Defaults tab.
3. From the Preview Type list, select Interactive Form.
4. Preview the form design in PDF:
   - Choose View→PDF Preview;
   - Or, on the Layout Editor, select the PDF Preview tab.
5. Test the form design:
   - Ensure that the form can be filled in using only the keyboard.
   - Ensure that all operations specified can be performed.
   - Ensure that all objects on the form are clearly visible.
6. Return to the Layout Editor:
   - Choose View→Body Pages;
   - Or, select the Body Pages tab.

Calculation Options

You can perform calculations in Adobe Designer using either FormCalc, the Native Adobe calculation language, or JavaScript.

FormCalc is the native Adobe calculation language that facilitates fast and efficient form design. It does not require a knowledge of traditional scripting techniques or languages. You can use the built-in functions of FormCalc to create forms quickly. The built-in functions available include mathematical, string, logical, date and time, web, and finance-related functions.

If you're familiar with the JavaScript programming language (which was originally designed to help create interactive web pages), you can add JavaScript code to form objects to further customize them. For example, JavaScript allows complex validation of field data to ensure that the respondent entered an appropriate value. You can use JavaScript to perform calculations in objects and to control actions. However, Adobe Reader doesn't support all JavaScript scripts, so you may want to restrict its use to documents others will view with Acrobat Standard or Acrobat Professional.

ACTIVITY 3-3

Creating Calculations

Activity Time:

10 minutes

Data Files:

- Spring05Classes.pdf

Scenario:

You've been asked to finish Super Fast Wheels' Spring05Classes.pdf document. The form is nearly complete, but needs the Total Cost object to calculate the total cost of the courses that a person is enrolled in.

What You Do	How You Do It
1. **Display the multiline version of the Script Editor.**	a. **Choose File→Open** to display the Open dialog box.
	b. **Click My Computer.**
	c. **Navigate to the C:\084173Data\Interactive PDF\Activity3\Start folder.**
	d. **Select the Spring05Classes.pdf file and click Open.**
	e. **Scroll down to view the Submit By Email button.**
	f. **Choose Window→Script Editor.**
	g. In the Script Editor, **position the mouse pointer above the Show drop-down list and double-click** to display the multiline version of the Script Editor.
	h. **Click and drag the Script Editor to the bottom of the Layout Editor** so that all objects on the Layout Editor are visible.
2. **Set the calculation to be triggered off on the object with the caption Total Cost.**	a. **Choose Edit→Lock Fields.**
	b. On the Layout Editor, **select the object with the caption Total Cost.**
	c. In the Script Editor, from the Show drop-down list, **select Enter.**
	d. In the Script Source Field, **type** ***TotalC=Sum(IntroC*75+AdvC*100)***
	e. **Click the Enter Script Source Changes button** to save the script.
	f. In the Script Editor, **click the Close button.**

3. **Adjust the tab order of the objects in the form.**

   a. **Choose View→Tab Order.**

   b. **Click OK** to dismiss the Tab Order message box.

   c. **Click the object with the caption Name** to change its Tab Order to 1.

   d. **Click the object with the caption Phone No** to change its Tab Order to 2.

   e. Similarly, **click the Address, Email, Credit Card No, No of Intro Courses, No of Adv Courses, Total Cost, and Submit By Email captions in sequence** to change their Tabbing Order.

   f. **Choose View→Tab Order.**

4. **Test the PDF form to ensure that the total cost is calculated as desired.**

    a. **Choose View→PDF Preview.**

    b. **Scroll down the form.**

    c. In the Name text box, **type *Anne Williams* and press Tab.**

    d. **Click No** to dismiss the Adobe Acrobat message box.

    e. **Type *310108552***

    f. **Press Tab and type *#4 Wallace Street***

    g. **Press Tab and type *anne@example.com***

    h. **Press Tab and type *4555 6788 5433 2345***

    i. **Press Tab and type *2***

    j. **Press Tab and type *1***

    k. **Press Tab** to view the total cost displayed in the Total Cost text box.

    l. **Press Tab** to verify that control is transferred to the Submit by Email button.

    m. **Choose View→Body Pages.**

    n. **Choose File→Save As.**

    o. **Click the Up One Level button.**

    p. **Double-click the Solution folder.**

    q. **Click Save.**

    r. **Close the File.**

    s. **Click Close** to dismiss the Welcome Screen.

TOPIC D

Create Fields with Predefined Responses

Text fields allow respondents to type unique responses. Another way for users to enter information is to choose from predefined responses. In this topic, you will create form fields with preset options.

Limiting user choices to a fixed number of responses saves respondents the time it would take to type their responses, ensures consistency, and makes data analysis easier.

Determine Which Form Field to Use

Guidelines

Each of the available form objects has its unique characteristics and limitations. Selecting the appropriate form fields will make your form much easier to use and to collect appropriate data. Use the following guidelines to choose form fields.

- Determine the type of data a user can enter—numeric or text. A Text Field object accepts textual data; a Numeric Field object accepts decimal or integer data.
- Determine if the respondent needs to select an item from a predefined list, or enter information on their own. If the user needs to select an item from a list, use a List Box object; use a Drop-down List object to enable the user to enter data manually if the option is not available in the list.
- Determine the number of items a user can select from a group of choices. Use a Radio Button object to select a single choice from a group of mutually exclusive choices; use a Check Box object to select one or more items from a group of choices.
- Determine the mode of return for the form. Use an Email Submit Button object if the form needs to be submitted to an email address; use a HTTP Submit Button object if it needs to be submitted to a specified URL.

Example:

You need to create a form for your client, to collect prospective customer names and personal information. The user's first name and last name needs to be collected, so you add Text Field objects. You decide to add a Drop-down List object to select a country from a list or allow the user to type in the country name not available in the list. The person responding can be a male or female so you decide to use the Radio Button object for the gender field. To enable the respondents to return the form data to a specified email address, you add an Email Submit Button object.

How to Create Fields with Predefined Responses

Procedure Reference: Create a Drop-down List

To create a drop-down list:

1. On the Library palette, double-click the Drop-down List object.

2. Reposition the object as needed.
3. On the Object palette, select the Binding tab
4. In the Name text box, specify a name for the drop-down list.
5. On the Object palette, select the Field tab and from the Appearance drop-down list, select the appropriate option.
   - None: Specifies that there will not be a border around the list.
   - Underlined: Underlines the list.
   - Solid Box: Displays a solid border around the list.
   - Sunken Box: Creates a three-dimensional effect by displaying a shadow around the list.
   - Custom: Displays the Custom Appearance dialog box, which can be used to give a customized look to the fillable area.
6. Add objects to the drop-down list:
   - Double-click in the Text text box, type the text for the list item to be added to the drop-down list, and press Enter;
   - Or, click the Add Item button, type the text for the list item to be added to the drop-down list, and press Enter.

   On the Binding tab of the Object palette, the Specify Item Values check box can be checked to specify custom data values for each list item.

7. Type the text for the next list item and press Enter.
8. Repeat step 7 to add as many items as needed.
9. When the list is complete, reposition items in the list individually by selecting the item you want to move, and clicking the Move Up or Move Down button.
10. If required, check Allow Custom Text Entry to type a selection that is not on the list.
11. On the Object palette, select the Value tab.
12. From the Type drop-down list, select the required option:
    - User Entered - Optional: Allows users to choose whether or not to enter data.
    - User Entered - Recommended: Can be set to display a custom message, if user does not enter data.
    - User Entered - Required: Can be set to display a custom message, if user does not enter data.
    - Calculated - Read Only: Calculates and displays a value through an attached script that the user will not be able to edit.
    - Calculated - User Can Override: User can edit the value calculated and displayed through an attached script.
    - Read Only: Displays a merged or calculated value at runtime that cannot be edited by the users.
13. From the Default drop-down list, select the default selection to be displayed on the drop-down list.

Procedure Reference: Create a List Box

To create a list box:

1. On the Library palette, double-click the Drop-down List Box object.
2. Reposition the object as needed.
3. On the Object palette, select the Binding tab.
4. In the Name text box, specify a name for the list box.
5. On the Object palette, select the Field tab and from the Appearance drop-down list, select the appropriate option.
    - None: Specifies that there will not be a border around the list.
    - Underlined: Underlines the list.
    - Solid Box: Displays a solid border around the list.
    - Sunken Box: Creates a three-dimensional effect by displaying a shadow around the list.
    - Custom: Displays the Custom Appearance dialog box, which can be used to give a customized look to the fillable area.
6. If required, on the Object palette, select the Field tab.
7. Add objects to the list box:
    - Double-click in the Text text box, type the text for the list item to be added to the drop-down list, and press Enter;
    - Or, click the Add Item button, type the text for the list item to be added to the drop-down list, and press Enter.

    On the Binding tab of the Object palette, the Specify Item Values check box can be checked to specify custom data values for each list item.

8. Type the text for the next list item and press Enter.
9. Repeat step 7 to add as many items as needed.
10. When the list is complete, reposition items in the list individually by selecting the item you want to move, and clicking the Move Up or Move Down button.
11. On the Object palette, select the Value tab.
12. From the Type drop-down list, select the required option:
    - User Entered - Optional: Allows users to choose whether or not to enter data.
    - User Entered - Recommended: Can be set to display a custom message, if user does not enter data.
    - User Entered - Required: Can be set to display a custom message, if user does not enter data.
    - Calculated - Read Only: Calculates and displays a value through an attached script that the user will not be able to edit.
    - Calculated - User Can Override: User can edit the value calculated and displayed through an attached script.
    - Read Only: Displays a merged or calculated value at runtime that cannot be edited by the users.

13. From the Default drop-down list, select the default selection that is to be displayed on the drop-down list.

Procedure Reference: Create Check Boxes

To create a check box:

1. On the Library palette, double-click the Check Box object.
2. Reposition the object as needed.
3. On the Object palette, select the Binding tab.
4. In the Name text box, specify a name for the check box.
5. On the Object palette, select the Field tab and from the Appearance drop-down list, select the appropriate option.
   - None: Specifies that there will not be a border around the check box.
   - Solid Square: Uses a solid square to represent the check box.
   - Sunken Square: Creates a three-dimensional effect by displaying a shadow around a square check box.
   - Solid Circle: Uses a solid circle to represent the check box.
   - Sunken Circle: Creates a three-dimensional effect by displaying a shadow around a circle check box.
   - Custom: Displays the Custom Appearance dialog box, which can be used to give a customized look to the fillable area.
6. Select one of the following options to specify the set of supported states for the check box:
   - On/Off: Specifies that the check box will be in either the selected or the clear state.
   - On/Off/Neutral: Specifies that the check box will be in selected, clear, or not in either selected or clear states.
7. If required, click in the Size text box and specify the size of the check box.
8. On the Object palette, select the Value tab.
9. From the Type drop-down list, select the required option:
   - User Entered: User can choose whether or not to check a check box.
   - Calculated - Read Only: Calculates and displays a value through an attached script at runtime. The user will not be able to edit this value.
   - Calculated - User Can Override: User can edit the value calculated and displayed through an attached script at runtime.
   - Read Only: Displays a merged or calculated value at runtime that cannot be edited by the users.
10. From the Default drop-down list, select the initial state of the check box.
11. Create additional check boxes by duplicating this check box and assigning each a different name.

Procedure Reference: Create Radio Buttons

To create radio buttons:

1. On the Library palette, double-click the Radio Button object.
2. Reposition the object as needed.
3. On the Object palette, select the Binding tab.
4. In the Name text box, specify a name for the radio button.
5. On the Object palette, select the Field tab and from the Appearance drop-down list, select the appropriate option.
   - None: Specifies that there will not be a border around the radio button.
   - Solid Square: Uses a solid square to represent the radio button.
   - Sunken Square: Creates a three-dimensional effect by displaying a shadow around a square radio button.
   - Solid Circle: Uses a solid circle to represent the radio button.
   - Sunken Circle: Creates a three-dimensional effect by displaying a shadow around a circle radio button.
   - Custom: Displays the Custom Appearance dialog box, which can be used to give a customized look to the fillable area.
6. If required, double-click the radio button caption displayed in the Item text box and change it.
7. On the Object palette, select the Value tab.
8. From the Type drop-down list, select the required option:.
   - User Entered - Optional: Allows users to choose whether or not to select an option.
   - User Entered - Recommended: Can be set to display a custom message, if user does not select an option.
   - User Entered - Required: Can be set to display a custom message, if user does not select an option.
   - Calculated - Read Only: Calculates and displays a value through an attached script that the user will not be able to edit.
   - Calculated - User Can Override: User can edit the value calculated and displayed through an attached script.
   - Read Only: Displays a merged or calculated value at runtime that cannot be edited by the users.
9. From the Default drop-down list, select the state in which the radio button is to be displayed.
10. If required, on the Object palette, select the Binding tab and check the Specify Item Values check box to specify custom On values for the radio buttons in that group. When this option is unchecked the On values will match the caption of the radio button. The default values are sequential integers starting at one.
11. Duplicate the initial radio button and give unique On values to each duplicate. Otherwise, selecting one radio button will not deselect the others automatically.

Procedure Reference: Align Objects to One Another

To align objects to one another:

1. Select the objects that you want to align.
2. Align objects to one another:
   - Choose Layout→Align→Left to align the left edges of the selected objects.
   - Choose Layout→Align→Right to align the right edges of the selected objects.
   - Choose Layout→Align→Top to align the top edges of the selected objects.
   - Choose Layout→Align→Bottom to align the bottom edges of the selected objects.
   - Choose Layout→Align→Vertical Center to align the vertical midpoints of the selected objects.
   - Choose Layout→Align→Horizontal Center to align the horizontal midpoints of the selected objects.

Procedure Reference: Align Objects Using the Layout Toolbar

To align objects to one another using the Layout toolbar:

1. Select the objects that you want to align.
2. Align objects to one another:
   - On the Layout toolbar, click the Align Left button to align the left edges of the selected objects.
   - On the Layout toolbar, click the Align Right button to align the right edges of the selected objects.
   - On the Layout toolbar, click the Align Top button to align the top edges of the selected objects.
   - On the Layout toolbar, click the Align Bottom button to align the bottom edges of the object.
   - On the Layout toolbar, click the Align Vertical Center button to align the vertical midpoints of the selected objects.
   - On the Layout toolbar, click the Align Horizontal Center button to align the horizontal midpoints of the selected objects.

Procedure Reference: Distribute Objects Evenly

To distribute objects evenly:

1. Select the objects that are to be distributed evenly.
2. Distribute objects evenly:
   - Choose Layout→Distribute→Across to distribute the objects evenly across the current selection area.
   - Choose Layout→Distribute→Down to distribute the objects evenly down the current selection area.
   - Choose Layout→Distribute→In Rows & Columns to distribute the objects evenly in rows and columns.

Procedure Reference: Distribute Objects Evenly Using the Layout Toolbar

To distribute objects evenly using the Layout toolbar:

1. Select the objects that are to be distributed evenly.
2. Distribute objects evenly:
   - On the Layout toolbar, click the Distribute Evenly Across button to distribute the objects evenly across the current selection area.
   - On the Layout toolbar, click the Distribute Evenly Down button to distribute the objects evenly down the current selection area.
   - On the Layout toolbar, click the Distribute Evenly In Rows And Columns button to distribute the objects evenly in rows and columns.

Procedure Reference: Align Objects to a Grid

To align objects to a grid:

1. Choose View→Grid.
2. If required, choose View→Snap To Grid to make items you move or resize stick to the grid.
3. Select the objects to be aligned.
4. Choose Layout→Align→To Grid.

Procedure Reference: Change the Display of Guidelines

To change the display of guidelines:

1. Choose View→Guidelines.
2. Position the mouse pointer on the top-left corner of the Layout Editor and click and drag to position the guideline at the required position.
3. If necessary, on the Drawing Aids palette, in the Grid & Ruler Settings section, click the Color drop-down arrow and select the desired color.
4. If necessary, in the horizontal ruler, click and drag the guideline triangle out of the Layout Editor to remove it.

Procedure Reference: Change the Display of the Object Boundaries

To change the display of the object boundaries:

1. Choose View→Object Boundaries.
2. On the Drawing Aids palette, next to the Show Object Boundaries check box, click the Color drop-down arrow and select the required color.

Grid and Guidelines

You may find it convenient to align items using the layout grid, which looks like a sheet of graph paper that overlays the page. You can use the grid to visually align items, and also to snap items so they align with the grid automatically. Choose View→Grid to show it and View→Snap To Grid to make items you move or resize stick to it.

You can also add guidelines, which are non-printing lines like gridlines. Guidelines can be placed wherever you want on the document. To create a guideline, choose View→Rulers, then drag from within the vertical or horizontal ruler into the Layout Editor. Choose View→Guidelines to toggle their display on or off.

Drawing Aids Palette

The Drawing Aids palette can be accessed by choosing Window→Drawing Aids. The Drawing Aids palette is used to specify the Layout Editor grid and ruler settings, and measurements. Rulers are displayed along the top and left side of the body or master page. Markers in the ruler display the position of the pointer as it moves. The origin of the ruler marks the grid's point of origin.

The Drawing Aids palette menu displays the commands for working with the Drawing Aids palette. This menu can be accessed by clicking the More button to the right of the palette. This table displays the commands and their description.

Command	Description
Help	Displays a description of the Drawing Aids palette by opening the Designer Help.
Hide Palette	Hides the palette.
Decimal Inches/Centimeters/Millimeters/Points	Displays the values as n in. or n cm.
Lines per Inch/Centimeters/Pica	Displays the values as n in. or n cm.
Guideline Sets	Adds horizontal and vertical guidelines.

You can modify the alignment of the objects by setting up grids and measurement units as required. You can use the Units drop-down list in the Grid & Ruler Settings section to specify the unit of measurement. The grid's origin can be changed by typing the coordinates in the X and Y Text Boxes in the Origin section. Similarly, the grid's interval can be changed by typing the coordinates in the X and Y Text Boxes in the Interval section. For example, if you set the origin to be 1 in and the interval to be 5 in, the grid would start at 1 in instead of at 0 and there would be 5 grid points displayed within an inch of space. Modifying the grids and measurement units would help you position objects precisely on the Layout Editor.

ACTIVITY 3-4

Adding Objects with Predefined Options to the Promotional Form

Activity Time:

10 minutes

Data Files:

- Spring05PromotionForm

Scenario:

Super Fast Wheels has branches only in the United States. However, since it's possible that respondents live in other countries, you want to add a Country object to the promotion campaign form to allow respondents to type a country name as well as to choose it from a list. In addition, you also need to know if the person owns a bicycle or not.

What You Do	How You Do It
1. **Create a drop-down list object for specifying the Country details. Format the font and set it to Arial, 12 point.**	a. **Choose File→Open** to display the Open dialog box.
	b. **Click My Computer.**
	c. **Navigate to the C:\084173Data\Interactive PDF\Activity4\Start folder.**
	d. **Select the Spring05PromotionForm.pdf file and click Open.**
	e. **Scroll down to view the Submit By Email button.**
	f. On the Library palette, **click the Drop-down List object.**
	g. On the Layout Editor, **click at the intersection of the 6.5-inch mark on the vertical ruler and the 3-inch mark on the horizontal ruler.**
	h. **Ctrl-click the object with the caption Email.**
	i. **Choose Layout→Make Same Size→Both.**
	j. **Click in a blank area of the form** to deselect the selected objects.
	k. **Select the drop-down list object.**
	l. In the Font toolbar, **click the Font Style drop-down arrow.**
	m. **Scroll up the drop-down list and select Arial.**
	n. In the Font toolbar, from the Font Size drop-down list, **select 12.**
	o. **Double-click in the caption part of the drop-down list and type *Country***

2.	**Name the drop-down list as ddCountry and make it a required field with the option of custom entry.**	a.	On the Object palette, on the Binding tab, **double-click in the Name textbox and type** ***ddCountry***
		b.	On the Object palette, **select the Value tab.**
		c.	From the Type drop-down list, **select User Entered - Required.**
		d.	On the Object palette, **select the Field tab.**
		e.	**Check Allow Custom Text Entry.**
3.	**Assign the values United States, Canada, and Mexico to the ddCountry object and make United States the default value.**	a.	**Click the Add Item button and type** ***United States***
		b.	**Press Enter and type** ***Canada***
		c.	**Press Enter and type** ***Mexico***
		d.	**Press Enter.**
		e.	On the Object palette, **select the Value tab.**
		f.	From the Default drop-down list, **select United States.**

4. **Create a check box object with the caption I Own A Super Fast Wheels Motorcycle.**

   a. On the Library palette, **click the Check Box object.**

   b. On the Layout Editor, **click at the intersection of the 7.5-inch mark on the vertical ruler and the 3-inch mark on the horizontal ruler.**

   c. **Ctrl-click the object with the caption Country.**

   d. **Choose Layout→Make Same Size→Both.**

   e. **Click in a blank area of the form** to deselect the selected objects.

   f. In the check box object, **position the mouse pointer in the boundary between the Field Value and the Field Caption to display the double-headed arrow.**

   g. **Click and drag towards the left till the boundary is in line with the boundary of the object with the caption Country.**

   h. **Format the font of the check box object and set it to Arial, 12.**

   i. **Double-click in the Caption part of the check box object and type *I Own A Super Fast Wheels Motorcycle***

---

5. **Name the check box object as cbCycle and make it a user-entered field.**

   a. On the Object palette, **select the Binding tab.**

   b. **Double-click in the Name textbox and type *cbCycle***

   c. On the Object palette, **select the Value tab.**

d. **Verify that the Type drop-down list is set to User Entered.**

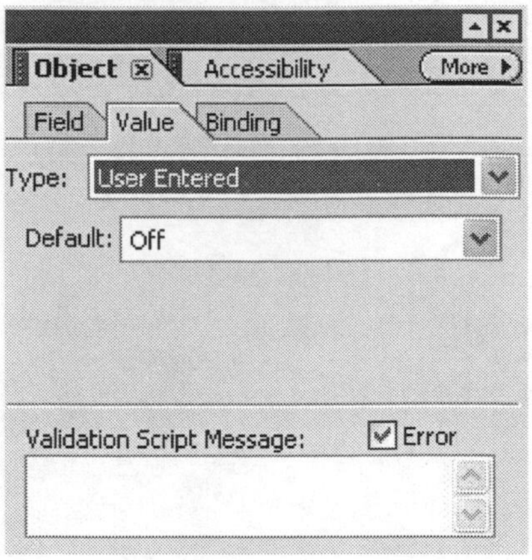

6. **Distribute the user-editable objects evenly.**

a. On the Layout Editor, **scroll up to view the object with the caption First Name.**

b. **Select the object with the caption First Name.**

c. **Hold down Ctrl and click the objects with the caption Last name, Comment, Email, Country, and I Own A Super Fast Wheels Motorcycle.**

d. **Choose Layout→Distribute→Down.**

e. **Choose File→Save As.**

f. **Click the Up One Level button.**

g. **Double-click the Solution folder.**

h. **Click Save.**

i. **Close the file.**

j. **Click Close** to dismiss the Welcome Screen.

7. **True or False? When the Specify Item Values check box is unchecked, the On values will match the caption of the radio button.**

__ True

__ False

TOPIC E

Create Buttons

You have provided several ways for respondents to work with a form. In this topic, you will use buttons to provide yet another method for the user to interact with the form.

Once a respondent has finished entering data into a form, they need to be able to click a button to submit the form to you so you can gather the information. Additionally, you might want to provide buttons that perform actions, such as clear the form data, or move to another document page or to a URL.

Form Submission Process

When users complete entering data into an electronic version of a form, they need to submit it so the form's creator can use the data they entered. The method the form designer uses for the form submission depends on the system for receiving and storing information that's been set up. The main stages of the form submission process are explained in Table 3-9.

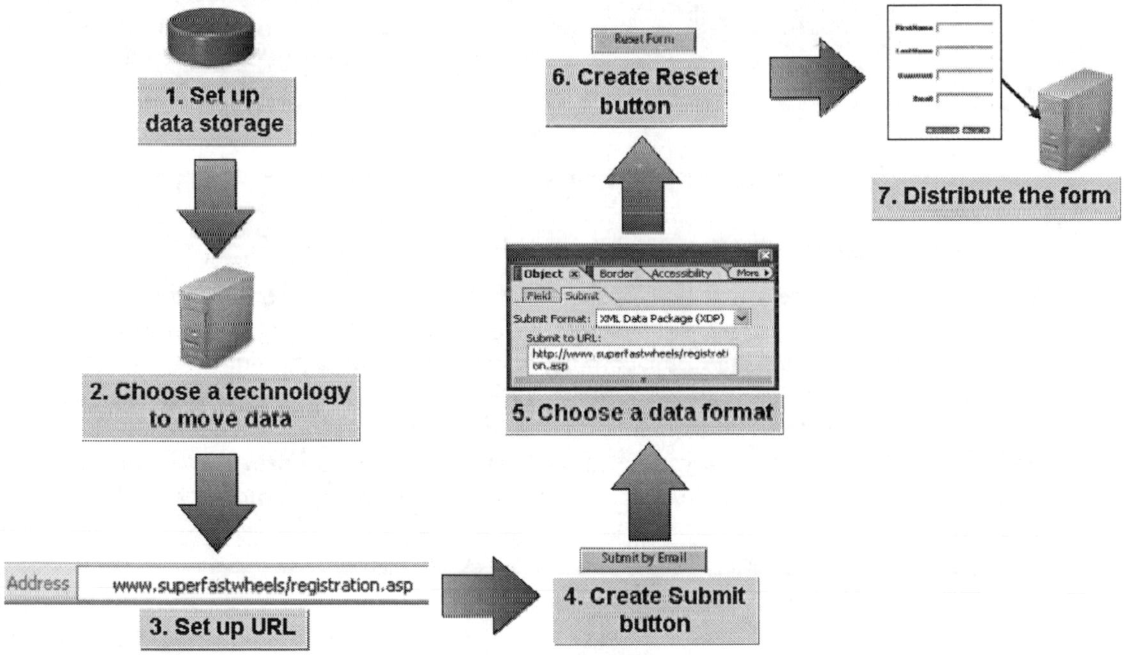

Table 3-9: *The stages of setting up a system for handling form submissions.*

Submit Format

The Submit tab appears in the Object palette, when you create a button and set its Control Type to Submit. The Submit tab provides several options (Table 3-10) specific to formatting buttons that submit data.

Table 3-10: *Options on the Submit tab*

Option	Description
Submit Format drop-down list	Specifies the format of the data to submit. • **XML Data Package (XDP)** Submits a package in the file format created by Designer. Select this format if the form initiates server-side processing, or to submit the form design, the form data, annotations, and all the other relevant information to the Form Server. • **PDF** Submits a package containing an embedded PDF file. Select this format if the form contains a signature field, or if a copy of the form together with its data needs to be saved by Form Server or submitted to some other target server. • **XML Data (XML)** Submits an XML data stream, which allows for the hierarchical representation of data. Select this format if the server that communicates with the run-time user application must receive an XML data stream. • **URL-Encorded Data (HTTP Post)** Submits a data stream to the specified Uniform Resource Locator (URL) using the POST method.
Submit To URL text box	Specifies the location of a web-hosted server. You can specify the ftp, http, https, or mailto protocol.

Form Data Collection Workflow

A workflow is a process that involves the automatic routing of form data, in a predefined sequence, among individuals and systems. If you have created a form with a Submit By Email button, the user completes the form, clicks the button, and the data is emailed back to you. You can consolidate the returned data into a spreadsheet. Alternatively, you can enable users to upload the entered data to Form Server. When the user clicks the Submit button at run time, the data is submitted to Form Server. Form Server can also be set up to forward the data to a custom application for further processing.

How to Create Buttons

Procedure Reference: Create a Button

To create a Button:

1. From the Library palette, select the Button object and place it on the Layout Editor.
2. Select the caption on the Button object and rename it as required.
3. On the Object palette, from the Appearance drop-down list, select the appropriate option:
    - No Border: Removes the line around the button.
    - Solid Border: Creates a thick line around the button.

- Raised Border: Creates a three-dimensional effect, by adding a shadow to the button.
- Custom: Displays the Custom Appearance dialog box, that can be used to give a custom look for the button.

4. In the Control Types listed, select the required option:
   - Regular: Executes the attached calculation or script.
   - Submit: Submits data according to the settings specified in the Submit tab.
   - Execute: Executes a web-service operation or database query according to the settings specified in the Execute tab.
5. If necessary, from the Presence drop-down list, select the appropriate option.
6. If necessary, specify the locale for language, using the Locale drop-down list.

The Submit Tab

The Submit tab is displayed when the Submit option is selected as the Control Type of a button. In the Submit tab, you can specify the format in which data will be submitted for processing. The available Submit Formats are listed below:

- XML Data Package (XDP): Submits a package in the format of the file in which it was created by Adobe Designer.
- PDF: Submits a package with an embedded PDF file.
- XML Data (XML): Submits an XML data stream that can be parsed by any generic XML parser.
- URL-encoded Data (HTTP Post): Uses the POST method to submit a text stream of text to the URL specified.

The Submit tab also provides the option to include annotations, PDF version of the form, digital signature, and a copy of the form without the merged data as attachments for the XDP files. You can also specify the encoding format for data transfers in this tab.

The Execute Tab

The Execute tab is displayed when the Execute option is selected as the Control Type for a button. The Execute tab provides you options specific to formatting buttons with a data connection. From the Connection drop-down, you can select the connection that is to be set, be it to a database or a WSDL file. The Connection Info section in this tab displays connection information and the operation or query to run. You can decide where an operation is to be performed, be it in the Client, Server or both Client and Server using the Run At drop-down list in the Execution Options. The Re-merge From Data check box allows you to specify whether or not the form structure needs to be updated after the processing completes.

Procedure Reference: Create a HTTP Submit Button

To create a HTTP Submit Button:

1. From the Library palette, select the HTTP Submit Button object and place it on the Layout Editor.
2. Select the caption on the object and rename it as required.
3. On the Object palette, from the Appearance drop-down list, select the appropriate option:

- No Border: Removes the line around the button.
- Solid Border: Creates a thick line around the button.
- Raised Border: Creates a three-dimensional effect, by adding a shadow to the button.
- Custom: Displays the Custom Appearance dialog box, that can be used to give a customized look to the button.

4. In the URL text box, specify the URL that the data will be sent to.
5. If required, set the border style for the button, using the Border palette.

Procedure Reference: Create a Print Button

To create a Print Button:

1. From the Library palette, select the Print Button object and place it on the Layout Editor.
2. Select the caption on the object and rename it as required.
3. On the Object palette, from the Appearance drop-down list, select the appropriate option:
    - No Border: Removes the line around the button.
    - Solid Border: Creates a thick line around the button.
    - Raised Border: Creates a three-dimensional effect, by adding a shadow to the button.
    - Custom: Displays the Custom Appearance dialog box, that can be used to give a customized look to the button.
4. If required, set the border style for the button, using the Border palette.

Procedure Reference: Create a Reset Button

To create a Reset Button:

1. From the Library palette, select the Reset Button object and place it on the Layout Editor.
2. Select the caption on the object and rename it as required.
3. On the Object palette, from the Appearance drop-down list, select the appropriate option:
    - No Border: Removes the line around the button.
    - Solid Border: Creates a thick line around the button.
    - Raised Border: Creates a three-dimensional effect, by adding a shadow to the button.
    - Custom: Displays the Custom Appearance dialog box, that can be used to give a customized look to the button.
4. If required, set the border style for the button, using the Border palette.

Procedure Reference: Create a Submit By Email Button

To create a Email Button:

1. From the Library palette, select the Submit By Email Button object and place it on the Layout Editor.

2. Select the caption on the object and rename it as required.
3. On the Object palette, from the Appearance drop-down list, select the appropriate option:
   - No Border: Removes the line around the button.
   - Solid Border: Creates a thick line around the button.
   - Raised Border: Creates a three-dimensional effect, by adding a shadow to the button.
   - Custom: Displays the Custom Appearance dialog box, that can be used to give a customized look to the button.
4. In the Email Address text box, specify the To address.
5. In the Email Subject text box, specify the subject for the mail. If this text box is not filled in, a default message is produced when the form is submitted.
6. If required, set the border style for the button, using the Border palette.

ACTIVITY 3-5

Creating Buttons

Activity Time:

5 minutes

Data Files:

- Spring05PromotionForm

Scenario:

The Spring05PromotionForm's design includes space at the bottom of the page for buttons the respondent can click to navigate and submit the form. Page 1 needs a Next Page button. You'll write code that will transfer control to the second page on the Click event of the button. You will then duplicate that button and edit it to create a Prev Page button on the second page.

What You Do	How You Do It
1. **Create a button with the caption Next Page at the bottom-right corner of page.**	a. **Choose File→Open** to display the Open dialog box. b. **Click My Computer.** c. **Navigate to the C:\084173Data\Interactive PDF\Activity5\Start folder.** d. **Select the Spring05PromotionForm.pdf file and click Open.** e. **Scroll down to the bottom of the first page.** f. On the Library palette, **click the Button object.** g. On the Layout Editor, **click at the intersection of the 8-inch mark on the vertical ruler and the 6.5-inch mark on the horizontal ruler.** h. **Double-click in the button object and type *Next Page*** i. **Click in a blank area of the Layout Editor** to deselect the selection. j. **Select the button object.** k. **Format the font of the button and set it to Arial, 12, Bold.**
2. **Attach a script to navigate to the next page in the button's click event.**	a. **Choose Window→Script Editor.** b. From the Show drop-down list, **select Click.** c. In the Script Source Field text box, **type *host.pageDown ()*** d. **Click the Enter Script Source Changes button.**

3. Duplicate the Next Page button and position it in the bottom-right corner of the second page.	a.	Choose Edit→Copy.
	b.	Scroll down to the second page of the form.
	c.	Click in the blank area next to the Submit By Email button on the second page.
	d.	Choose Edit→Paste.
	e.	Drag the duplicate button to the right of the Submit By Email button.
4. Change the caption of the duplicate Button object to Prev Page and attach a script to navigate to the previous page in the button's click event.	a.	Double-click in the duplicate button and type *Prev Page*
	b.	In the Script Source Field text box, click before host, hold down Shift and click after ().
	c.	Type *host.pageUp ()*
	d.	Click the Enter Script Source Changes button.
	e.	Close the Script Editor.
5. Save the changes and test the PDF form to check if the buttons work as desired.	a.	Choose File→Save As.
	b.	Click the Up One Level button.
	c.	Double-click the Solution folder.
	d.	Click Save.
	e.	Select the PDF Preview tab.
	f.	Scroll down and click the Next Page button.
	g.	Scroll down and click the Prev Page button.
	h.	Select the Body Pages tab.
	i.	Choose File→Exit.

TOPIC F

Organize Collected Data in a Spreadsheet

When you begin to receive form submissions, you need to gather the data for analysis. In this topic, you will organize collected responses in a spreadsheet.

PDF forms act as a conduit to pass on user responses to you. Manually extracting responses submitted by email can take a lot of time and effort on your part. Acrobat enables you to create a spreadsheet file from received forms, organizing the data in a logical and useful manner.

Form Data Options

On the File→Form Data menu, there are a number of commands (Table 3-11)which can be used to analyze the information collected through the forms.

Table 3-11: *Form Data options*

Command	Description
Initiate Data File Collection Workflow	This command opens a wizard which initiates an email-based Form Data Collection workflow. The first step is to email your form to the users. Then, the respondents will fill out the form and send it back to you. The form data will be collected in data files.
Create Spreadsheets From Data Files	This command allows you to integrate the information collected in the data files into a spreadsheet.
Import Data To Form	This command allows you to select a data file from which information will be imported to a form.
Export Data From Form	This command stores the information entered by a respondent in a form in a data file.

How to Organize Collected Data in a Spreadsheet

Procedure Reference: Export Form Data

To export form data:

1. In Acrobat, in the Tasks bar, click the Forms drop-down arrow and choose Create Spreadsheet From Data Files.
2. In the Export Data From Multiple Forms dialog box, click Add Files.
3. In the Select File Containing Form Data dialog box, select the files you want to export.
4. Click Select.
5. In the Export Data From Multiple Forms dialog box, click Export.

6. In the Select Folder To Save Comma Separated File dialog box, in the File Name text box, type a name.
7. Click Save.
8. In the Export Progress dialog box, click View File Now.
9. Close Excel without saving the file.
10. In the Export Progress dialog box, click Close Dialog.

ACTIVITY 3-6

Exporting Form Data to a Spreadsheet

Activity Time:

5 minutes

Setup:

No files are open.

Scenario:

You had been asked to conduct a survey among all the Super Fast Wheels company employees on a picnic organized by the company. You've surveyed all employees using the Company Picnic Survey form that you had created. You have collected the required data in XML files and want to display the results in an organized format that you can easily manipulate. You decide to export the data to a spreadsheet in Excel.

What You Do	How You Do It
1. **Export the five consecutively numbered Company Picnic Survey.xml files to a spreadsheet.**	a. **Choose Start→All Programs→Adobe Acrobat 7.0 Professional.**
	b. In the Tasks bar, **click the Forms drop-down arrow and choose Create Spreadsheet From Data Files.**
	c. In the Export Data From Multiple Forms dialog box, **click Add Files.**
	d. **Click My Computer.**
	e. **Navigate to the C:\084173Data\Interactive PDF\Activity6\Start folder.**
	f. **Select the Company Picnic Survey1.xml file, hold down Shift, and select Company Picnic Survey5.xml file.**
	g. **Click Select.**
	h. **Click Export.**
	i. In the File Name text box, **type *Picnic Data***
	j. **Click the Up One Level button.**
	k. **Double-click the Solution folder.**
	l. **Click Save.**

2. **View the exported file as a spreadsheet in Excel and then close Excel.**

   a. In the Export Progress dialog box, **click View File Now.**

   b. **Expand the width of the first five columns** to view the details in them.

   c. **Scroll to the right and expand the remaining columns** to view the details in them.

   d. **Close Excel.**

   e. In the Microsoft Excel dialog box that is displayed, **click No.**

   f. In the Export Progress dialog box, **click Close Dialog.**

Lesson 3 Follow-up

In this lesson, you created interactive forms with text fields, fields with predefined options, buttons, and calculations. These skills will enable you to create PDF documents in which viewers can respond with valuable feedback.

1. **What types of forms would you want to make?**

2. **Which form objects do you anticipate being most useful for increasing the usability of the forms you create?**

NOTES

LESSON 4

Preparing PDF Files for Commercial Printing

Lesson Time
80 minutes

Lesson Objectives:

In this lesson, you will begin preparing a PDF document for commercial printing.

You will:

- Examine the commercial printing process.
- Choose an appropriate method to create a PDF file for prepress.
- Display color accurately when viewing a PDF document.
- Create a set of appropriate Adobe PDF Settings for prepress.
- Preview a proof for color separations, transparency, and overprinting.

Introduction

If you need to print many copies of a PDF document, you should have it commercially printed. In this lesson, you will begin preparing PDF files for commercial printing.

By generating prepress-friendly PDF documents, you may only need to transfer one file per document to the print vendor, rather than having to gather and send all of the associated graphic and font files for each. You can also preview colors and printed effects on screen for problems. These reviews will help avoid the need for reprints, save time and money.

TOPIC A

Examine the Commercial Printing Process

Before preparing PDFs to be sent to a commercial printer, you should have a basic understanding of commercial printing. In this topic, you will examine the commercial printing process.

Understanding the commercial printing process will help you generate prepress-friendly PDF documents. The print vendor will appreciate the simplicity and the reliability of the jobs you send, since you would have checked for problems prior to handoff, and you'll save money and time by preventing costly reworks.

Color Separation

Definition:

Color separation is the process of dividing colors into ink components for the purpose of printing each ink separately. Each color separation is a grayscale representation of where one color ink is to be applied to the page. Color separations are usually output to a film instead of paper, which is used to create a printing plate.

Example:

Color Page

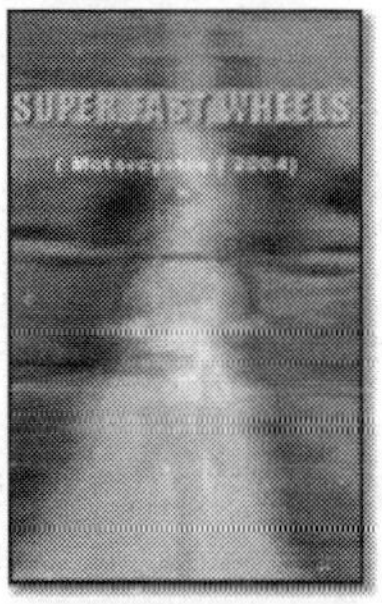

Cyan Plate

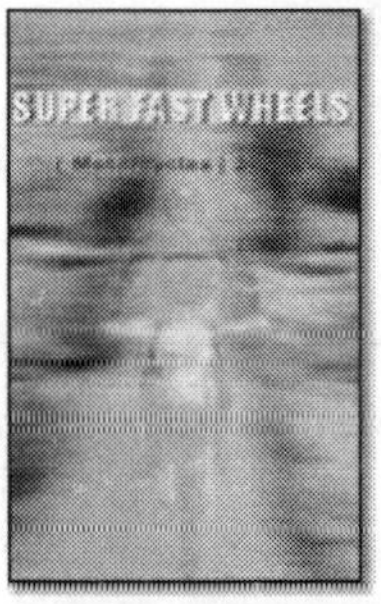

Magenta Plate

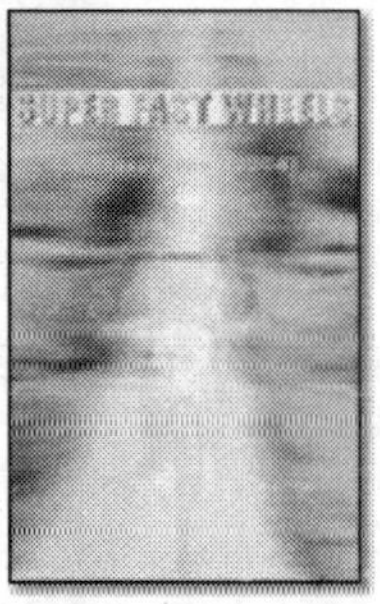

Yellow Plate

Black Plate

Trapping

Definition:

Trapping is the process of ensuring that adjoining color areas overlap slightly to prevent white gaps from appearing between colors. During commercial printing, when paper passes through a printing press, each ink is applied separately, one after another. If the paper shifts or stretches, the inks may not align perfectly with one another. This can cause ugly white gaps between adjoining colors or unwanted underlying colors showing through. You can use traps to create a slightly overprinting edge where the inks intersect. The width, appearance, placement, and thresholds of a trap can be changed.

Example:

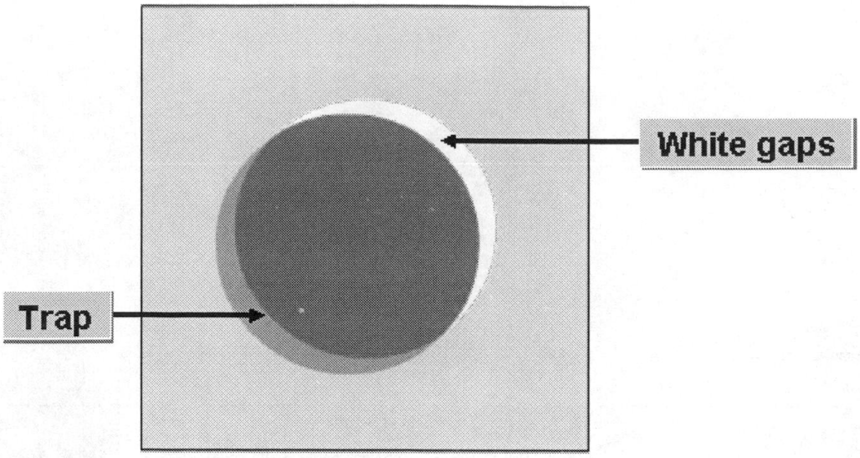

Types of Traps

There are two types of traps: a spread, in which a lighter object overlaps a darker background and seems to expand into the background; and a choke, in which a lighter background overlaps a darker object that falls within the background and seems to squeeze or reduce the object.

Color Printing

All color printing is produced by using one or more color components. Depending on the complexity of the document, you may use as few as one or as many as six or more inks. If the pages contain full color photographs, the document must be printed with at least four colors: (CMYK) cyan, magenta, yellow, and black. Some color printers use additional inks to allow for a broader range, or gamut, of colors, but all use at least the CMYK colors.

Composite Color Printing

Definition:

Composite color printing is the process of printing to a device that outputs directly to a page. During composite printing, all of the color inks are combined onto the finished medium at once. Composite printers, such as desktop printers or color copiers, are usually used for low print quantities and as proofs for publications that will be commercially printed.

Example:

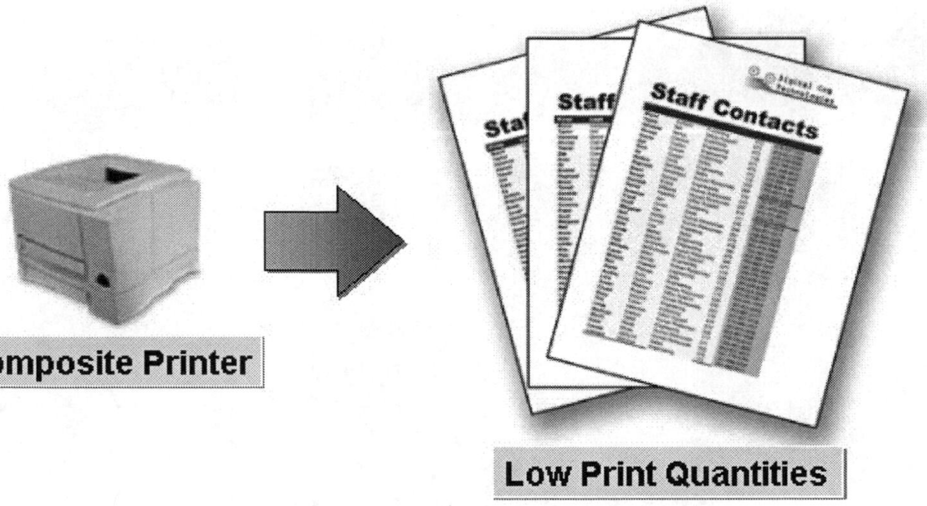

When to Use Commercial Printing

Guidelines

While composite printing is often a wise choice, some print jobs are better achieved by sending the document to a commercial printer. Choosing the right approach will help you achieve the print quality you want at an affordable price. You should consider getting a document commercially printed if:

- You need hundreds or thousands of copies. The cost per page of commercial printing is much lower than that of desktop printing, although you need to print a larger number of pages to make up for the large setup cost. Also, a vendor may be able to print a large quantity faster than you could achieve using a desktop printer.
- You need pages bound into a book.
- You need a paper larger than letter or tabloid size.
- You need to *bleed* color to the edges of the paper or print on both sides of a page (although some desktop printers can do these, it's usually not convenient, particularly at high quantity).
- You need to print packaging materials, such as labels.
- You want to ensure high, consistent quality for all of the prints.

Example:

As a graphic designer, you have been asked to design and print thousands of copies of a company's annual report, with color bleeds on each edge. You should send your document to a commercial printer rather than print this using the composite printer in your office.

The Commercial Printing Process

When you choose to send a document to a print vendor to be printed on a press, the process is much more complicated than composite printing. The main stages of commercial printing process are explained in Table 4-1.

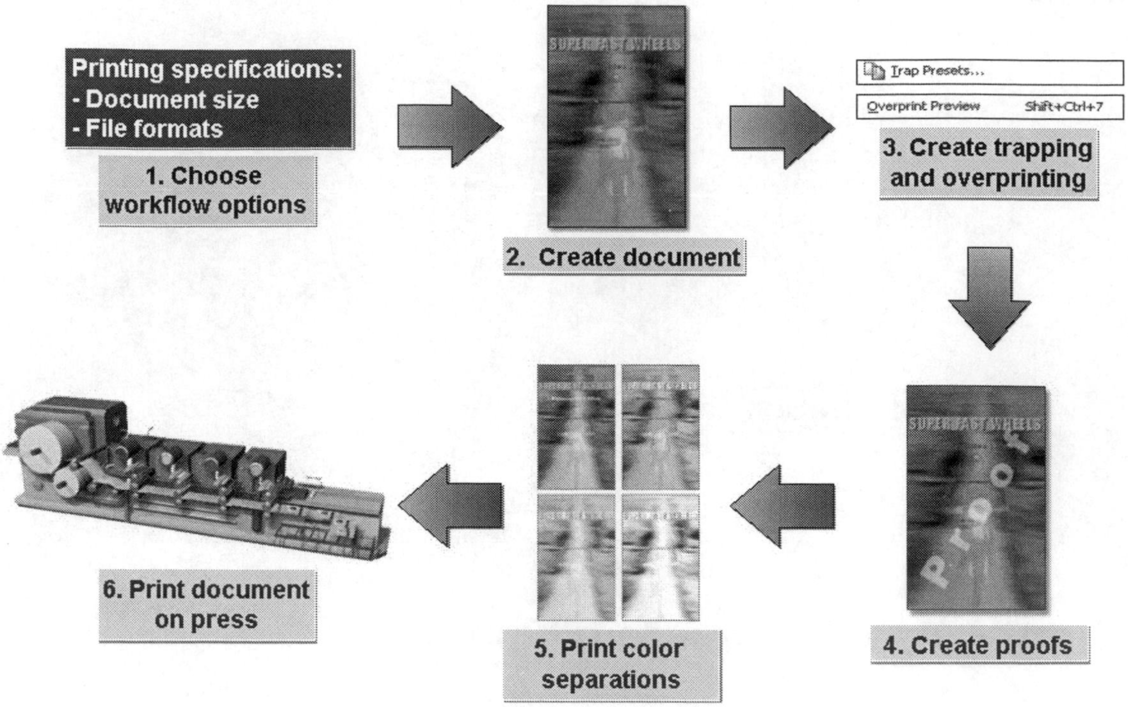

Table 4-1: *Stages of the commercial printing process*

Stage	Description
Choose workflow options	Define printing specifications (press, paper stock, and so on), document size, file formats (application and font files, PDF, or PostScript, and so on), who's responsible for what (color issues, trapping, and so on). Typically, the designer and the print vendor are the parties involved in this stage.
Create document	The designer creates the document based on workflow options chosen.
Create trapping and overprinting	Creating trapping and overprinting are often necessary for quality commercial printing, and may be created within the document, as a part of the prepress work by the print vendor, or during print time.
Create proofs	Proofs are prints that show how the final document is intended to look. Depending on the accuracy requirement, the designer may print proofs or may ask the print vendor to provide them.
Print color separations	This allows the printer to create a printing plate for each ink. It's typically done by the print vendor, but the designer may print color separations as proofs or generate the actual separations to provide to the printing company.
Print document on press	The print vendor prints the document, including any necessary binding and packaging.

Transparency

Definition:

Transparency is any editable area within a document that is less than completely opaque. Objects in the background are partially or fully visible through transparent objects. You can create transparency using the opacity controls in many design applications. When you reduce an object's opacity, you are increasing its transparency.

Example:

ACTIVITY 4-1

Describing Commercial Printing

Activity Time:

5 minutes

Scenario:

You have a set of print jobs, for which you plan to use a commercial printer instead of a composite printer. Before moving forward, it is time to review your knowledge on the subject.

What You Do	How You Do It

1. **Arrange in sequence the different stages of the commercial printing process.**

    Print color separations

    Create trapping and overprinting

    Create proofs

    Print document on press

    Choose workflow options

    Create document

2. **Which process divides colors into ink components for printing each ink separately?**

    a) Color separation

    b) Trapping

    c) Composite color printing

    d) Transparency

3. **True or False? Objects in the background are partially or fully visible through transparent objects.**

    __ True

    __ False

TOPIC B

Choose Appropriate Methods of Creating PDF Files for Prepress

Not all PDFs are appropriate for creating commercial printing files. In this topic, you will choose methods that generate PDF files that will work as intended when handed off to a print vendor.

If you choose a method of creating PDF files that isn't appropriate for prepress use, the files will be unusable by the print vendor for creating high-quality prints. You'll either have to regenerate and send a PDF file they can use, or accept lower quality if there's not enough time to do the rework. Choosing the appropriate prepress method of creating PDF files will allow the print vendor to produce high-quality output.

Approaches to Color Separation in a PDF Workflow

When you use a PDF workflow, the stage at which color separation occurs affects how you generate the PDF file. There are three basic approaches to create color separations as explained in Table 4-2.

Table 4-2: *Approaches to create color separations*

Approach	Description
Submit a PDF with CMYK and spot colors.	You submit a PDF file that contains CMYK and spot colors, and the print vendor generates the color separated film or color plates without having to perform any color mode conversions. Many vendors will insist on this approach, since it prevents unexpected shifts in color from what you saw on screen in RGB.
Submit a PDF with RGB colors.	You submit a PDF file that contains RGB colors, and the print vendor creates the color separations themselves. This allows them to choose how the RGB colors are converted to CMYK, using a profile for their specific press and possibly accounting for issues such as their expected dot gain (the amount the ink spreads as it is absorbed into the paper). However, images may have unwanted color shifts and may not achieve as good a quality as you could get by fine-tuning images in CMYK yourself.
Generate a color-separated PDF file.	You generate a PDF file that's already color separated, with each page representing an individual color plate. Rather than the document appearing in composite color, each page will appear as a grayscale version of where a certain ink will be applied. Most print vendors will probably prefer to create the color separations themselves, so they can benefit from seeing the composite color on screen. Acrobat can produce color separations, so there's not much benefit to sending pre-separated files to a vendor. However, you may benefit from creating separations for your own viewing, so you can ensure that the inks are applied as you expect.

Trapping in a PDF Workflow

There are two basic approaches to applying trapping.

- Apply trapping within the application that creates the files. Although most professional publishing applications, such as QuarkXPress, Adobe InDesign, Illustrator, and Photoshop, offer approaches for trapping artwork, it can be tedious and time-consuming ensuring that all the objects will trap correctly to one another. The more objects you have that partially overlap, contain gradients, and contain raster art, the more difficult it is to trap your files.
- Allow the printing vendor to use dedicated trapping software. The printing vendor will use an application on native application files, files they generate (PDF, Postscript, or EPS files), or will apply in-RIP trapping that works with any file format and creates the traps as part of imaging the document to film or printing plates.

Transparency Flattening in PDF Documents

When transparent objects are printed, or when a document is converted to a PDF in a format compatible with Acrobat 4 or earlier, they need to be flattened, because PDF formats prior to PDF 1.4 do not directly handle transparency. *Flattening* is a technology that blends overlapping objects, which have transparency applied to them, into one flat set of opaque objects. During flattening, the software finds areas where transparent objects overlap other objects and divides the objects into components.

Flattener Preview

The Flattener Preview dialog box allows you to apply flattener settings, preview them, and apply them to the PDF document. Transparency flattener settings are listed in Table 4-3.You can find the objects that are transparent and the objects that will be affected by transparency flattening. Transparent objects are highlighted in red and the rest of the document objects appear in grayscale.

Table 4-3: *Transparency flattener settings*

Transparency Flattener Setting	Description
Raster/Vector Balance	Determines whether objects with transparency are rasterized when it is converted into output or maintained as vector objects. When the slider is set closer to the Vectors end, less rasterization will be performed on the file's graphics. This is dependent on the complexity of the file and the variety of objects included in the transparency flattening.
Line Art And Text Resolution	Sets the resolution of objects that are rasterized when the file is flattened. The objects that are rasterized could include images, vector artwork, text, and gradients. Resolution values can range from 72 ppi to 2400 ppi.
Gradient And Mesh Resolution	Sets the resolution for gradients and meshes when the file is flattened. Values in the range of 72–2400 ppi can be specified. Higher settings may not increase the quality of the output.
Convert All Text To Outlines	Ensures that when transparent text objects are flattened, the width of text characters remains consistent.
Convert All Strokes To Outlines	Maintains stroke width consistency between stroke objects that contain transparency and those that do not.
Clip Complex Regions	Eliminates color stitching, which results when the rasterization of complex graphics causes pixels to be rendered in a blocked or stitched fashion.
Preserve Overprint	Creates an overprint effect by blending the color of transparent artwork with the background color.

How to Choose the Method to Create PDF Files for Prepress

Choosing an appropriate method to generate PDF files for use in a prepress workflow ensures high quality printing, and prevents costly rework when you submit PDF files to a commercial print vendor.

Guidelines

The following methods are capable of producing PDF documents for prepress:

1. **Print from an application directly to PDF:** You can maintain the high quality of the image, by specifying the appropriate Adobe PDF document properties. You can also choose the named settings you created in Acrobat Distiller, which allows you to set any possible option that you desire.
2. **Print a PostScript file and distill it manually:** As with prior versions of Acrobat, you can still use the two-step process of printing to PostScript or EPS, and then running Acrobat Distiller separately to create a PDF file. In most cases, this approach is unnecessary. However, some situations may require it. For example, your prepress provider may prefer to distill PostScript files using their own settings, or you may want to convert multiple PostScript files to PDF via a watched folder or customized process.
3. **Export or Save As PDF from an application:** Many publishing applications allow you to use an Export or Save As command to generate PDF files. Most of these applications provide customized dialog boxes with PDF options that are similar or identical to those in the Adobe PDF Settings dialog box within Distiller. Some include extra options, such as the ability to automatically create links from table of contents entries to the corresponding document pages. As long as you choose these settings properly, these applications should create PDF files that work well in a prepress workflow.

You should avoid the following methods to create a PDF document when it's to be used for prepress:

1. **Converting web pages to a PDF document:** While you can convert a file from the Internet to PDF, the image quality won't be sufficient for high-resolution printing. These methods create 72 pixel per inch RGB images, but images for commercial printing should typically be around 300 ppi.
2. **Converting Scanned pages to a PDF document:** You can scan paper documents directly to PDF. This method treats each page as a single image, which severely limits flexibility even if you achieve a good scan.
3. **Open As Adobe PDF:** You can convert BMP, CompuServe® GIF, HTML, JPEG, PCX, PNG, Text, or TIFF files to PDF, using the Create PDF command menu in the Tasks toolbar. As such, this command cannot accept files from professional layout or illustration applications. In prepress, this command can be used only to print a single high-resolution image, but there are other better ways to do so.

Example:

You want to create a PDF file from a Photoshop image that you want printed for commercial purposes. You can create the PDF file by printing from the application directly to the PDF, or by using the Save As command and saving it as a PDF file.

ACTIVITY 4-2

Choosing the Method to Create a PDF File for Prepress

Activity Time:

5 minutes

Data Files:

- Magazine Ad Comp.jpeg
- Magazine Ad PS.psd

Scenario:

You need to create a prepress-ready PDF file of an advertisement that is to be printed in a magazine. Another designer has emailed you a JPEG file composite of the document Magazine Ad Comp.jpeg as well as the document created in Photoshop application Magazine Ad PS.psd. You now need to decide on a method to create the PDF file to be sent to the commercial printer.

What You Do	How You Do It

1. **Which of the following methods are appropriate for creating the PDF file for prepress purposes?**

   a) Open the Magazine Ad PS.psd document in Photoshop, and print directly to PDF.

   b) In Acrobat, generate a pdf file of the Magazine Ad PS.psd file using the Create PDF drop-down list on the Tasks toolbar.

   c) Open the Magazine Ad PS.psd document, and generate the PDF file by saving directly to PDF in the Save As dialog box.

   d) Print a postscript file and distill it manually.

2. **Convert the JPEG file composite to PDF from within Acrobat.**

   a. On the Tasks toolbar, **click Create PDF and choose From File.**

   b. **Click My Computer.**

   c. **Navigate to the C:\084173Data\Commercial Printing\Activity2\Start folder.**

   d. **Select the Magazine Ad Comp.jpeg file and click Open.**

   e. **Click OK** to dismiss the Adobe Acrobat message box.

   f. From the Zoom drop-down list, **select 400.**

   g. **Scroll down to view the text.**

   h. **Click the Save button.**

   i. **Navigate to the C:\084173Data\Commercial Printing\Activity2\Solution folder and click Save.**

---

3. **What makes the PDF file generated from the JPEG file composite inappropriate for prepress.**

   a) It is entirely composed of a raster image

   b) Includes vector art

   c) Contains gray colored pixels around the characters of the body text

   d) Includes text

---

4. **Generate a PDF using the original file created in Photoshop.**

   a. **Close the file.**

   b. **Choose Start→All Programs→Adobe Photoshop 7.0.1.**

   c. **Choose File→Open.**

   d. **Click My Computer.**

   e. **Navigate to the C:\084173Data\Commercial Printing\Activity2\Start folder.**

   f. **Select the Magazine Ad PS.psd file and click Open.**

   g. **Choose File→Print.**

   h. In the Adobe Photoshop message box, **click Proceed.**

   i. From the Name drop-down list, **select Adobe PDF.**

   j. **Click OK.**

   k. **Navigate to the C:\084173Data\Commercial Printing\Activity2\Solution folder and click Save.**

   l. From the Zoom drop-down list, **select 400.**

   m. **Scroll down and to the right.**

   n. **View the text and then close the file.**

   o. **Minimize the Adobe Acrobat Professional window.**

   p. In the Adobe Photoshop window, **choose File→Exit.**

   q. **Restore the Adobe Acrobat Professional application.**

TOPIC C

Apply Color Management Settings

If your PDFs contain color, you can refine the process of creating PDFs for commercial printing. In this topic, you will apply color management settings.

Every monitor and printer displays color differently. If the colors seem different on different devices, you cannot be sure that the commercially printed output will look reasonable. Applying color management can help ensure that colors will match as accurately as possible when displayed on different devices.

Color Management

Definition:

Color Management is an option in the Preferences dialog box that is used to make colors match consistently between a computer monitor and a printer's output. You can adjust the RGB, CMYK, or Grayscale working spaces and select a predefined color management setting.

Successful color management requires a device-independent color space that transforms colors from one color space to another and an accurate profiling to describe a color behavior of a digital color device.

Example:

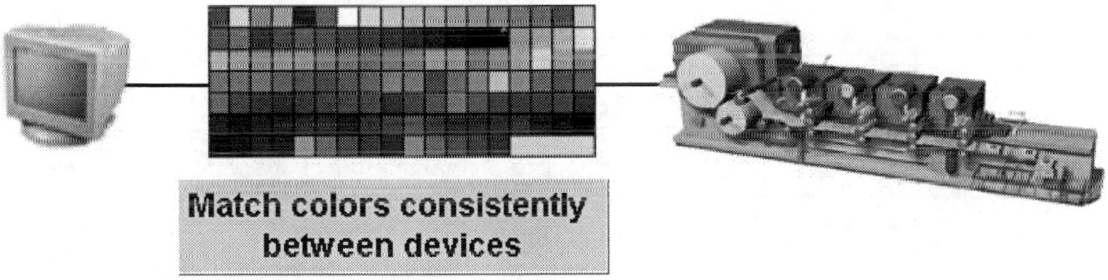

The Color Management Process

To properly implement color management, you need to establish a workflow that ensures consistency. Table 4-4 describes the basic stages of the color management process.

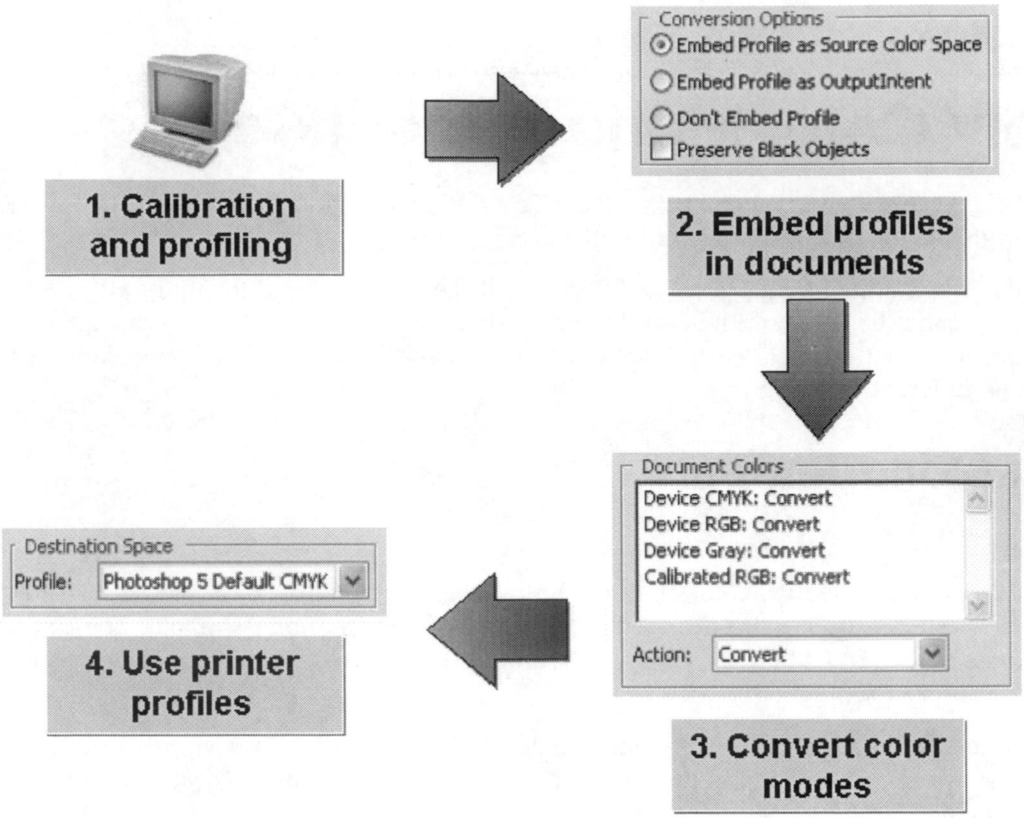

Table 4-4: *Stages of a color management workflow*

Stage	Description
Calibration and profiling	Color management begins with calibrating each device you use (monitors and printers) to ensure consistency. You can use a third-party utility such as the Adobe Gamma control panel or a combination of software and hardware calibration tools. When the calibration is complete, the software saves the characteristics of the display (also referred to as its color space) to a file, called an International Color Consortium (ICC) profile, on your hard disk. Each application that employs color management can read and interpret color spaces, and will convert colors as necessary to account for differences between the color space currently in use and the one used by each file's creator.
Embed profiles in documents	When a person corrects color or adjusts images (in RGB with an application, such as Photoshop), they should choose to embed a profile within the image file. This profile represents the color space in which they are viewing the file. This step ensures that all document colors indicate the color space of origin, so they can be properly transformed when displayed on other devices.
Convert color modes using profiles	Images are typically created in RGB but printed in CMYK. While the designer usually converts the image, it may be done as late as during printing.

Stage	Description
Use printer profiles during printing	To get accurate matches on multiple printers, the person printing should choose the appropriate printer profile, so the application converts colors from the embedded profile(s) to that of the printer. Typically the designer uses a printer profile that represents the color of the print vendor's device (as closely as possible), and the print vendor also applies a color profile for their output device when printing.

Color Management Control

If you choose to employ color management, you will find that much of it happens behind the scenes in Acrobat. For example, if you open a document with embedded ICC profiles, it will automatically read those profiles, and will attempt to match the original colors, converting them as necessary based on the differences between your monitor and the creator's. However, there are two aspects of color management that you can control in Acrobat:

- **How colors of existing PDF files are displayed and printed.** When you open a PDF document that does not have color management profiles embedded, Acrobat will assume a color space that was used to create the document to display its colors accurately. You can set the default color spaces for RGB and CMYK colors to match the color spaces you expect will be used most often. The color space choice affects how Acrobat displays the colors on your monitor, and how they will print from your computer.
- **Color management settings used to convert a document to PDF.** When you generate a PDF document from the original content, you can control many options for the representation of colors. For example, you can choose to convert all colors to CMYK, and can choose whether or not to embed color profiles.

How to Apply Color Management Settings

Procedure Reference: Apply Color Management Settings

To apply color management:

1. Choose Edit→Preferences.
2. In the Categories list box, select Color Management.
3. From the Settings drop-down list, select the appropriate configuration to display the specific color management settings associated with it.
4. From the RGB, CMYK, and Grayscale drop-down lists, select the color space with which you expect untagged documents to have been created.
5. If you want a document's embedded Output Intent information (which is different from an embedded ICC profile, and is created when the PDF file is generated or edited in Acrobat) to take precedence over the working color space you chose, check the Output Intent Overrides Working Spaces check box.
6. Click OK to close the Preferences dialog box.

ACTIVITY 4-3

Applying Color Management Settings

Activity Time:

5 minutes

Data Files:

- Catalog 2004 Print.pdf

Scenario:

You have received the Catalog 2004 Print.pdf file that was created by some other designer for review. You are not sure if that designer included embedded ICC profiles. You want to make sure that images in the catalog file display in Acrobat as it were seen by the designer.

What You Do	How You Do It
1. **Compare the appearance of the background with Acrobat's default RGB color space set to Apple RGB, sRGB, and Adobe RGB (1998).**	a. **Choose File→Open.**
	b. **Click My Computer.**
	c. **Navigate to the C:\084173Data\Commercial Printing\Activity3\Start folder.**
	d. **Select the Catalog 2004 Print.pdf file and click Open.**
	e. **Choose Edit→Preferences.**
	f. In the Categories list box, **select Color Management.**
	g. From the RGB drop-down list, **select Apple RGB.**
	h. **Click OK.**
	i. **Observe the color of the background in the catalog file and then choose Edit→Preferences.**
	j. From the RGB drop-down list, **select sRGB IEC61966-2.1 and click OK.**
	k. The green color of the background darkens. **Choose Edit→Preferences.**
	l. **Click the RGB drop-down arrow.**
	m. **Scroll up the RGB drop-down list and select Adobe RGB (1998).**
	n. **Click OK.**

2. **Choose the U.S. Prepress Defaults color management setting and close the file.**	a. The green color of the background appears more saturated. **Choose Edit→Preferences.**
	b. From the Settings drop-down list, **select U.S. Prepress Defaults.**
	c. **Click OK.**
	d. **Close the file.**

TOPIC D

Create and Apply Appropriate Adobe PDF Settings for Prepress

Perhaps the most critically important aspect of generating a prepress-friendly document is selecting appropriate Adobe PDF settings. In this topic, you will create and apply a set of appropriate PDF settings that will ensure high-quality printed output.

Adjusting and saving your own named set of Adobe PDF Settings will help ensure that your document will work properly for your print vendor.

Acrobat Distiller 7.0

Acrobat Distiller lets you create PDF files from other file formats. You can select the settings to be used when converting documents to PDF files. You can also edit the default settings and save them. You can distribute this settings file to other computers and users to ensure consistent PDF creation. In the Acrobat Distiller window, you can open PostScript files for conversion to PDF files, choose font locations and watched folders, and set security for the PDF files.

Color Settings

The Color panel of the Adobe PDF Settings dialog box allows you to choose settings that affect how document colors are retained, converted, and characterized (profiled) in the PDF document you create.

Choose Color Management Policies to do one of the following with colors:

- Leave colors unchanged.
- Tag all colors for color management.
- Tag only images for color management.
- Convert all colors to the sRGB color space (profile).
- Convert all colors to the CMYK color space (profile).

To simplify the options you choose, Acrobat combines the above choice with other options, such as which color spaces to use for grayscale, RGB, and CMYK, into settings you can select from the Settings File drop-down list. For example, if you choose the U.S. Prepress Defaults settings file, it automatically selects Tag Everything For Color Management from the Color Management Policies drop-down list, and uses working color spaces appropriate for commercial printing. Further simplifying things, most Settings File choices prevent you from changing the settings below, so you only choose from one menu to control several options.

Relationship Between the Adobe PDF Printer and Distiller

You can convert files in an authoring application, such as InDesign, to PDF using the Print command. The Print command uses the Adobe PDF printer to convert the source document to a PostScript file and is fed directly to Distiller for conversion to PDF, without manually starting Distiller. By default, the last used Acrobat 7.0 Distiller settings file is used to create the PDF file, but you can select a specific Distiller settings file either from within the creation application or under Properties in the Print dialog box when printing.

How to Create and Apply Adobe PDF Settings for Prepress

Procedure Reference: Create a Named Set of Adobe PDF Settings

To create a named set of Adobe PDF settings:

1. Choose Advanced→Acrobat Distiller.
2. From the Default Settings drop-down list, select the existing set that best matches the settings you want to create.

   The Press Quality setting is the best one to use as a model for creating prepress settings.

3. Choose Settings→Edit Adobe PDF Settings.
4. Select the General folder to specify file options such as Adobe PDF file compatibility and binding, and to set a default page size for EPS files.
5. Select the Images folder to specify resolution, compression, and image quality settings that can reduce the file size required for images within a PDF document.
6. Select the Fonts folder to specify the fonts to embed.
7. Select the Color folder to specify Adobe Color Settings, Color Management Policies, and Working Spaces.
8. Select the Advanced folder to choose options that control the conversion from PostScript to PDF, and to choose which Document Structuring Conventions to retain in the PDF document.
9. Select the Standards folder to specify settings necessary to create PDF files that comply with the PDF/X or PDF/A standard.
10. Click OK to save the settings in the existing settings file.
11. Save the revised settings:

- Click Save As, navigate to the Shared Documents\Adobe PDF\Settings folder, and click Save to make the revised settings appear in the Adobe PDF Settings drop-down list.
- Or, click Save As, enter a name and location for the new file, and click Save.

General Options

Choosing settings in the Adobe PDF Settings dialog box to match yours and your print vendor's specifications will allow you to generate PDF documents that print at high quality without problems. Most of the options in the General folder of the Adobe PDF Settings dialog box isn't critical for prepress work; the resulting PDF file will likely be fine, regardless of the settings.

Option	Description
Compatibility	Set the compatibility level of the Adobe PDF by selecting the appropriate option from the Compatibility drop-down list. You should always choose as high a PDF version as possible (in this case version 1.6). If you are creating a PDF file that will be widely distributed, you can use Version 1.3 (Acrobat 4.0) or Version 1.5 (Acrobat 5.0) to ensure that all users can view and print the document, if required. Version 1.2 isn't recommended; it has limited page size; doesn't support ICC color management; patterns and masked images may not display properly and it can't accept double-byte (Kanji) fonts.
Object Level Compression	Object Level Compression consolidates small objects that are not compressible by themselves into streams of data that can be compressed efficiently. The Off option can be used if you do not want to compress any structural information in the PDF document. The Tags Only option can be used if you want to compress structural information in the PDF.
Auto-Rotate Pages	Auto-Rotate Pages automatically rotates pages based on the orientation of the text or DSC comments. You can choose either to rotate pages individually based on the direction of the text on that page or collectively based on the orientation of the majority of text.
Binding	While the Binding option may appear important, it only affects the on-screen display in Acrobat's Continuous-Facing view and not the physical binding of the printed document.
Resolution	Similarly, the Resolution setting doesn't affect the quality of the PDF file (the PDF format doesn't have an inherent resolution). It's only necessary for PostScript processing, and doesn't affect image resolution or downsampling.
All Pages/Pages From	Use the All Pages or Pages From options to specify the pages to convert to Adobe PDF.
Embed Thumbnails	While it's not strictly necessary to embed thumbnails for sending a file to a commercial printer, some prefer to have them for preflighting. For example, thumbnails can help a print provider see at a glance whether page orientation is off and whether bleeds exist.

Option	Description
Optimize For Fast Web View	The Optimize For Fast Web View option restructures the file for one-page-at-a-time downloading from the web servers. This would allow faster access and display of the file when it is downloaded from the web or a network.
Default Page Size	Lastly, Default Page Size only matters when the PostScript file that Distiller is processing doesn't specify a page size (which can occur with output from QuarkXPress, for example).

Image Options

The Images options allow you to compress and downsample color, grayscale, and monochrome images:

Option	Description
Downsample	Downsamples images that have a significantly high resolution; the resampling process blurs images slightly. To do this, set the For Images Above value significantly higher than the Bicubic Downsampling To value. An image with a significantly high resolution probably won't cause printing problems, but one that's been downsampled unnecessarily can look worse than it should. The different options for downsampling includes: Average Downsampling To, Subsampling, and Bicubic Downsampling. The Average Downsampling option averages the pixels in a sample area and then replaces the entire downsampling area with the color in the sampled area at the specified resolution. The Subsampling option chooses a pixel in the center of the sample area and replaces the entire downsampling area with the color of that pixel. This method results in images that are less smooth and discontinuous. The Bicubic Downsampling To option the pixel color by calculating a weighted average and then replaces the entire downsampling area with that color. This method is more effective than the Average Downsampling method.
Compression	Choose an appropriate compression method. The ZIP option works well on monochrome, color, or grayscale images with large areas of the same color or pattern. The JPEG color applies compression on grayscale or color images that contain more detail than can be reproduced on screen or in print. The Automatic method usually does a good job; It automatically determines the best quality for color and grayscale images and applies that color to the images. The JPEG and Automatic compression options are not available for monochrome images. It includes other options such as CCITT Group 4, CCITT Group 3, and Run Length.
Image Quality	The Image Quality can be set to Minimum, Low, Medium, High, and Maximum for both Color and Grayscale images.
Anti-Alias To Gray	The Anti-Alias To Gray option for monochrome images allows you to smooth jagged edges. You can choose between 2, 4, or 8 bits to specify 4, 16, and 256 levels of gray. This option may make small letters and thin lines blurred.

Option	Description
Policy	The Policy button can be clicked to specify the image processing methods when the image is below the resolution you have defined. In the Image Policy dialog box, you need to specify the resolution of the image and the action to be taken when the image is below that resolution. The action that could be taken includes Ignore, Warn And Continue, and Cancel Job.

Font Options

The Font options can be used to specify the fonts that are to be embedded in an Adobe PDF file. You can also choose whether or not to embed a subset of characters used in the PDF file.

Option	Description
Embed All Fonts	Check the Embed All Fonts check box to make sure that all the fonts used in the document will be included in the file itself. This will ensure that the document will print properly even if the print provider doesn't have the fonts you used.
Subset Embedded Fonts When Percent Of Characters Used Is Less Than	This option can be used to specify a threshold value when there is a need to embed only a subset of a font. This keeps the file size down while still embedding the characters used in the document. Some type foundries require subsetting fonts rather than embedding entire fonts in their licensing agreements, and subsetting reduces the file size slightly.
When Embedding Fails	The When Embedding Fails option can be used to specify how the Distiller should respond if it is unable to locate a font for the file that it is processing. Selecting either the Warn And Continue or Cancel Job options ensures that you don't overlook a PDF file thinking that fonts are embedded in it.
Embedding	When you embed subsets of fonts less than 100%, the settings at the Embedding section are irrelevant; the fonts will always be embedded as subsets, without exception.

Color Options

You should always apply the settings as per your printing company's recommendations. In general, you should use a Settings file such as U.S. Prepress Defaults rather than one intended for on-screen display (such as Web Graphics Defaults).

Option	Description
Settings File	The only Settings File option that allows you to individually change the drop-down lists below is None; you should use it if you wish to exercise more control over color management than with a preset. When you choose None, you can assign a profile to the file's colors so it accurately reflects the color space in which you edited colors. If you use the None setting to customize the choices below, you shouldn't use the Convert All Colors To sRGB color management policy. The sRGB color space has too small a gamut for high-quality commercial print work; it's intended for displaying images through the web.
Color Management Policies	Select from the Color Management Policies drop-down list based on your color management setup • If you or your printing vendor have calibrated all of your devices and have chosen colors based on that (for example, using printed proofs) rather than based on color management profiles, select Leave Color Unchanged to retain the color values you originally chose. • If you use color management for images and for choosing colors for other items such as fonts and solid colors, select Tag Everything For Color Management and choose Acrobat 4.0 or 5.0 Compatibility in the General Adobe PDF Settings tab. This will embed ICC profiles in the document for each image. • If you use color management for images only (for example, within Photoshop), select Tag Only Images For Color Management. This embeds ICC profiles in images only, preventing color shifts in text and graphics. You may need to use this option to avoid color changes to black text.
Working Spaces	Choose working spaces that most likely represent any images without embedded profiles or document colors that aren't color managed.
Preserve Under Color Removal And Black Generation	You should generally check the Preserve Under Color Removal And Black Generation check box; It controls how colors are converted from RGB to CMYK.
When Transfer Functions Are Found	If any of the EPS images contain a transfer function to map it to a specific printer, and you intend to print to that device, select Preserve or Apply from the When Transfer Functions Are Found drop-down list; for printing to any device, select Remove.
Preserve Halftone Information	If any of the EPS images contain halftone information intended for a specific printer, and you intend to print to that device, check the Preserve Halftone Information check box; uncheck it otherwise.

Other Adobe PDF Settings Options

In most cases, you can use the default settings in Advanced Options. The only reason to change any of them would be per exact instructions from your print provider that they need for their specific applications and workflow.

If you need to ensure PDF/X compliance, select the PDF/X-1a or PDF/X-3 options from the Compliance Standard drop-down list in the Standard Options. If you want to preserve files for long term use, select PDF/A.

ACTIVITY 4-4

Creating a PDF Settings File

Activity Time:

10 minutes

Data Files:

- Magazine Ad PS.psd

Scenario:

You send the advertisements you prepare to a particular magazine. Since you send advertisements to them regularly, it makes sense to save a custom Adobe PDF setting in Distiller, so you can use it every time you send an advertisement to that magazine. You want to create a setting that minimizes the file size, while retaining high quality when printed with a 133 lpi halftone screen. Additionally, you want all the advertisements you prepare to adhere to U.S. prepress defaults, with all CMYK images, and without transfer functions.

What You Do	How You Do It
1. **Launch Acrobat Distiller and select the Press Quality PDF setting.**	a. **Choose Advanced→Acrobat Distiller.** b. From the Default Settings drop-down list, **select Press Quality.**
2. **Edit the Images options of the Press Quality setting so that color and grayscale images over 350 pixels-per-inch are downsampled to 266 pixels-per-inch by using the Bicubic method.**	a. **Choose Settings→Edit Adobe PDF Settings.** b. **Select the Images folder.** c. In the Color Images section, next to the Downsample drop-down list, **double-click in the text box and type *266*** d. In the Color Images section, **double-click in the For Images Above text box and type *350*** e. In the Grayscale Images section, next to the Downsample drop-down list, **double-click in the text box and type *266*** f. In the Grayscale Images section, **double-click in the For Images Above text box and type *350***

3. **Apply the U.S. Prepress Defaults color setting with transfer functions removed.**	a. **Select the Color folder.** b. From the Settings File drop-down list, **select U.S. Prepress Defaults.** c. From the When Transfer Functions Are Found drop-down list, **select Remove.**
4. **Save the customized settings as a PDF setting file in the default Settings folder.**	a. **Click Save As.** b. In the File Name text box, **type *Magazine 133 lpi, CM*** c. **Click Save.** d. **Click OK.** e. In the Acrobat Distiller dialog box, **click the Close button.**
5. **Launch Adobe Photoshop and open the Magazine Ad PS.psd file.**	a. **Choose Start→All Programs→Adobe Photoshop 7.0.1.** b. **Choose File→Open.** c. **Click My Computer.** d. **Navigate to the C:\084173Data\Commercial Printing\Activity4\Start folder.** e. **Select the Magazine Ad PS.psd file and click Open.**

6. **Print the Photoshop file to a PDF using the customized settings.**

   Be sure to choose the Print command, not the Print With Preview command, which you would select if you used the common keyboard shortcut Ctrl+P.

   a. **Choose File→Print.**
   b. In the Adobe Photoshop message box, **click Proceed.**
   c. From the Name drop-down list, **select Adobe PDF.**
   d. **Click Properties.**
   e. **Click Add.**
   f. In the Paper Names text box, **type *Magazine Ad***
   g. **Double-click in the Width text box and type *8.13***
   h. **Double-click in the Height text box and type *10.88***
   i. **Click Add/Modify.**
   j. From the Default Settings drop-down list, **select Magazine 133 lpi, CM.**
   k. **Click OK** to return to the Print dialog box.
   l. **Click OK** to close the Print dialog box.
   m. In the File Name text box, **type *Magazine Ad PS Evaluation.pdf***
   n. **Navigate to the C:\084173Data\Commercial Printing\Activity4\Solution folder and click Save** to generate the PDF file.
   o. **Close the file.**
   p. **Minimize the Adobe Acrobat Professional window.**
   q. In the Adobe Photoshop window, **choose File→Exit.**
   r. **Restore the Adobe Acrobat Professional application.**

Topic E

Preview Printed Effects on Screen

Once a PDF document has been created for prepress, you and/or the print vendor may want to preview it to make sure that it will print correctly on the press. In this topic, you will preview printed effects on screen.

By previewing the document on screen as it will appear when printed, you can save money, as well as the time required to print a test document.

Output Preview Options

Using the Output Preview window, you can preview separations, proof colors, view colors by source, and highlight warning areas. Some of the options in the Output Preview window are explained in Table 4-5.

Table 4-5: *Options in the Output Preview window*

Option	Description
Simulation Profile	Indicates the color profile of a specific output device.
Simulate Ink Black	Check this option to preview the actual dynamic range defined by the proof profile.
Simulate Paper White	Check this option to preview the specific shade of white exhibited by the print medium described by the proof profile. Checking this option automatically checks the Simulate Ink Black option.
Ink Manager	Is used to remap the spot color inks to equivalent CMYK process colors. Ink Manager settings affect how inks will be print when separations are generated and how inks are viewed using Output Preview.
Show	The Show drop-down list is used to select a color space to be viewed.
Preview	Is used to choose whether to preview separations or color warnings.
Show Overprinting	Indicates how blending, transparency, and overprinting will appear in a color-separated output. This is useful for proofing color separations.
Rich Black	Indicates areas that will print as process black (K) ink mixed with color inks for increased opacity and rich color. Rich-black objects knock out the colors beneath, preventing background objects showing through.

Simulation Profile Settings

You can select a color profile from the Simulation Profile drop-down list (Table 4-6). It is important to understand when to use which profile.

Table 4-6: *Simulation Profiles*

Profile	Description
Adobe RGB (1998)	Provides a fairly large gamut of colors and is well suited to documents that will be converted to CMYK. Use this space if you need to do print production work with a broad range of colors.
Apple RGB	Reflects the characteristics of the Apple Standard 13-inch monitor and is used by a variety of desktop publishing applications, including Adobe Photoshop 4.0 and earlier. Use this space for files that you plan to display on Mac OS monitors, or for working with legacy (older) desktop publishing files.
ColorMatch RGB	Matches the native color space of Radius Pressview monitors. This space provides a smaller gamut alternative to Adobe RGB (1998) for print production work.
sRGB IEC61966-2.1	Reflects the characteristics of the average computer monitor. This standard space is endorsed by many hardware and software manufacturers, and is becoming the default color space for many scanners, low-end printers, and software applications. This space is recommended for web work, but not for prepress work (because of its limited color gamut).
Euroscale Coated v2	Produces high-quality separations using Euroscale inks under the following printing conditions: 350% total area of ink coverage, positive plate, bright white coated stock.
Euroscale Uncoated v2	Produces high-quality separations using Euroscale inks under the following printing conditions: 260% total area of ink coverage, positive plate, uncoated white offset stock.
Japan Color 2001 Coated	Produces high-quality separations using Japan Color inks under the following printing conditions: 350% total area ink coverage, positive film, ISO Type 3 paper.
Japan Color 2001 Uncoated	Produces high-quality separations using Japan Color inks under the following printing conditions: 310% total area ink coverage, positive film, ISO Type 4 paper.
Japan Color 2002 Newspaper	Produces high-quality separations for newspaper printing using Japan Color inks under the following conditions: 230% total ink coverage, positive film, standard newsprint paper in Japan.
Japan Web Coated (Ad)	Produces high-quality separations based on the following printing conditions: 320% total area ink coverage, positive film. This profile was created using the JMPA (Japan Magazine & Printing Association) data sets. Data sets are based on DDCP (Digital) proofing standards.
U.S. Sheetfed Coated v2	Produces high-quality separations using U.S. inks under the following printing conditions: 350% total area of ink coverage, negative plate, bright white coated stock.
U.S. Sheetfed Uncoated v2	Produces high-quality separations using U.S. inks under the following printing conditions: 260% total area of ink coverage, negative plate, uncoated white offset stock.

Profile	Description
U.S. Web Coated (SWOP) v2	Produces high-quality separations using U.S. inks under the following printing conditions: 300% total area of ink coverage, negative plate, coated publication-grade stock. This profile was created using the TR001 characterization data.
U.S. Web Uncoated v2	Produces high-quality separations using U.S. inks under the following printing conditions: 260% total area of ink coverage, negative plate, uncoated white offset stock.
Dot Gain 10%	Represents the color space that reflects the grayscale characteristics of a dot gain. Dot gain occurs when a printer's halftone dots change as the ink spreads and is absorbed by paper.
Gray Gamma 1.8	Matches the default grayscale display of Mac OS computers and is also the default grayscale space for Photoshop 4.0 and earlier.
Gray Gamma 2.2	Matches the default grayscale display of Windows computers.

Separations Preview

The Separations section in the Output Preview window displays the four process plates and the spot plates. When only one process separation is selected, Acrobat displays it as a grayscale image. You can hide a separation by unchecking the box to the left of the separation name. You can also hide or view all the process or spot colors. The Total Area Coverage specifies the total percentage of all the inks used.

Overprint Preview

The Overprint Preview mode provides an on-screen simulation of how blending and overprinting will appear in a printed output. When you have three overlapping objects, it will be impossible to determine how their color will look in the output. Turning on the Overprint Preview mode gives you a clear idea as to how these colors will look when printed.

Highlight Options

While you are previewing transparency flattening, you can use the Highlight drop-down list to select the objects to be highlighted. The highlight options are listed in Table 4-7.

Table 4-7: *Options in the Highlight drop-down list*

Option	Description
Rasterized Complex Regions	Highlights complex vector areas that will be converted to rasters when flattened.
Transparent Objects	Highlights objects that contain transparency.
All Affected Objects	Highlights transparent objects and their underlying objects.
Expanded Patterns	Highlights patterned areas that will be expanded to individual objects when flattened.

Option	Description
Outlined Strokes	Highlights strokes that will be converted to outlines when flattened.

How to Preview Printed Effects on Screen

Procedure Reference: How to Preview Printed Effects on Screen

To preview printed effects on screen:

1. Choose Advanced→Output Preview.
2. Preview how the document's colors would appear when printed on a specific printer using one of the following methods:
   - Check Simulate Ink Black to make the on-screen display simulate the actual dynamic range defined by the proof profile.
   - Check Simulate Paper White to make the on-screen display simulate the specific shade of white exhibited by the print medium described by the proof profile. Checking this option automatically checks the Simulate Ink Black option.
   - If both Simulate Ink Black and Simulate Paper White are unchecked you can simulate only the ink black or paper white simulation without simulating a different proof file.
3. If necessary, view separation plates using one of the following methods:
   - In the Separations section, uncheck the box to the left of the separation name to hide that separation.
   - In the Separations section, check the empty box to the left of each separation name to view that separation.
   - In the Separations section, check or uncheck the box to the left of the Process Plates or Spot Plates separations, to toggle between viewing and hiding all process or spot colors.
4. Choose Advanced→Overprint Preview to preview overprinting. Only documents created with the PDF 1.4 (Acrobat 5) or PDF 1.5 (Acrobat 6) format can display overprinting on screen.

Procedure Reference: Transparency Flattening

1. Choose Tools→Print Production→Transparency Flattening.
2. If required, click in the Preview area, press the Spacebar and drag to pan the preview.
3. From the Highlight drop-down list, select the appropriate option.
4. Specify appropriate Flattener Settings.
5. If required, in the Preview Settings section, click Refresh to display a fresh preview of the image based on the settings selected.
6. In the Apply To PDF section, select one of the following options and click Apply to apply the changes to the Adobe PDF document:

- All Pages In Document: Applies the settings to all the pages in the document.
- Current Page: Applies the settings to the page that is currently visible in the document.
- Pages Range: Applies the settings to the range of pages specified in the From and To text boxes.

The availability of options in the Highlight drop-down list depends on the content of the artwork and the Transparency Flattening settings specified in the Advanced Print dialog box.

ACTIVITY 4-5

Previewing Printed Effects on Screen

Activity Time:

10 minutes

Data Files:

- Catalog 2004 Print.pdf

Scenario:

You're working with the Super Fast Wheels' catalog file that is being readied for prepress. You're considering whether to print it on coated or uncoated stock, so you want to preview it as it will appear printed with the U.S. Web Coated (SWOP) V2 and U.S. Web Uncoated V2 standards. You want to look at each color plate for potential problems. In addition, you want to determine the transparent objects, the objects affected by transparency, and the Raster/Vector balance value at which the vector areas with complex transparency will be rasterized.

What You Do	How You Do It
1. **Proof the catalog file using both the coated and uncoated color spaces, opting for the one with the more saturated color appearance.**	a. **Choose File→Open.** b. **Click My Computer.** c. **Navigate to the C:\084173Data\Commercial Printing\Activity5\Start folder.** d. **Select the Catalog 2004 Print.pdf file and click Open.** e. **Choose Advanced→Output Preview.**

f. In the Simulation Profile drop-down list, **verify that U.S. Web Coated (SWOP) V2 is selected and then observe the color of the background.**

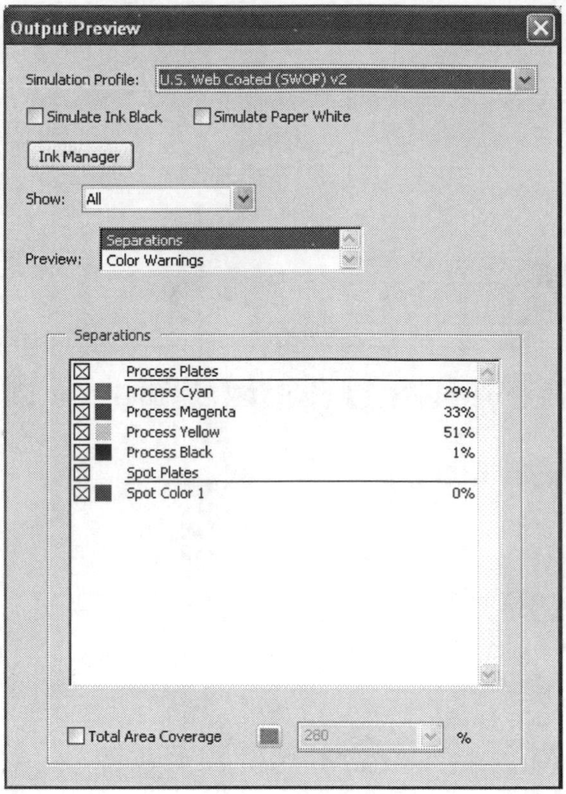

g. From the Simulation Profile drop-down list, **select U.S. Web Uncoated V2.**

h. The image colors look less vibrant when Acrobat simulates the document's appearance as printed on uncoated stock. **Click the Simulation Profile drop-down arrow.**

i. **Scroll up and select U.S. Web Coated (SWOP) V2.**

2. **On the first page, preview the color separation plates as progressive builds and look for possible printing problems.**

   a. **Uncheck Process Plates.**

   b. **Uncheck Spot Plates.**

   c. **Check Process Cyan.**

   d. The Cyan plate appears in grayscale, since you're viewing one plate only. **Check Process Magenta.**

   e. The combination of the plates appears in color. **Check Process Yellow.**

   f. **Check Process Black.**

   g. **Check Spot Plates.**

   h. The color appears complete with all color plates checked. **Close the Output Preview dialog box.**

3. **Preview transparency flattening settings on the third page.**

a. On the status bar, **click the Single Page button.**

b. **Scroll down to page 3.**

c. **Choose Tools→Print Production→Transparency Flattening.**

d. From the Highlight drop-down list, **select Transparent Objects** to highlight in red the transparent objects.

e. **Click Refresh.**

f. From the Highlight drop-down list, **select All Affected Objects** to highlight in red the underlying objects that are affected.

g. **Click Refresh.**

h. **Click and drag the Raster/Vector Balance slider to the 50% mark.**

i. **Click Refresh.**

j. **Click the Highlight drop-down arrow.**

k. The Rasterized Complex Regions option is still grayed out. **Click the Highlight drop-down arrow** to accept the default selection.

l. **Click and drag the Raster/Vector Balance slider to the 20% mark.**

m. **Click Refresh.**

n. From the Highlight drop-down list, **select Rasterized Complex Regions.**

o. **Close the Flattener Preview dialog box.**

p. **Close the file.**

Lesson 4 Follow-up

In this lesson, you used appropriate methods to generate PDF files for commercial printing. The ability to generate prepress-friendly PDF files will ensure high quality and save you time and money when handing them off to a commercial printer.

1. **Which techniques will you find most valuable in preparing files for commercial printing? Why?**

2. **Which settings in the Advanced Print Setup dialog box are most important to get your desired printed output? Why?**

NOTES

LESSON 5
Finalizing PDF Files for Commercial Printing

Lesson Time
65 minutes

Lesson Objectives:

In this lesson, you will create composite and color separation prints from a PDF document.

You will:

- Preflight documents intended for commercial printing.
- Create a PDF/X-compliant PDF file.
- Print a composite of a PDF document.
- Print color separations of a PDF document.

Introduction

Once you have prepared and previewed a PDF document for commercial printing, you will need to generate the file that will actually be sent to the print vendor. In this lesson, you will create and test PDF documents to ensure successful printed output.

Just because a document displays well on a monitor, does not necessarily mean there won't be printing problems. Just like previewing documents on screen, testing and generating compliant files can help avoid the need for costly vendor intervention and potential reprints, saving time and money.

TOPIC A

Preflight Documents

Another technique you can use to help prepare a document for commercial printing is to test it for potential printing problems. In this topic, you will use Acrobat to preflight a PDF document.

While all of the techniques you have used so far are valuable for creating and viewing a PDF document that is targeted for commercial printing, none of them can ensure that a document doesn't contain potentially problematic elements. You can search a document and identify such hard-to-find elements, including items incompatible with a particular workflow and elements that could result in poor quality, extra expense, or a complete failure to print.

Rules and Conditions

A *condition* is a simple statement that is either true or false for a given object in a PDF document. Rules govern almost any aspect of the document, including document properties and image properties. Rules allow you to group multiple conditions together.

Preflight Profiles

Definition:

A *preflight profile* is a set of criteria that defines acceptable values for a document. A preflight profile must contain at least one rule and one condition that validate the Adobe PDF content. You can add or remove conditions from rules, and rules from profiles. Preflight profiles can be shared with other users. You can prevent unauthorized changes to preflight profiles by locking profiles and giving them passwords.

Example:

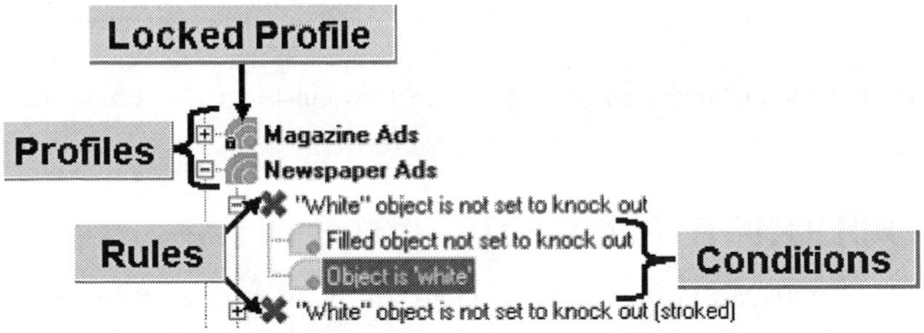

Preflight Alerts

An alert icon appears next to each rule that was violated according to the selected Preflight profile. There are four types of alerts as shown in Table 5-1.

Table 5-1: *Preflight alerts*

Alert	Description
	Error generates an error message for a rule. Choose this option for mismatches that must be corrected before the PDF document can continue to the next stage in the workflow.
	Warning generates a warning message for a rule. Choose this option for mismatches that you want to know about and may need to correct before final output.
	Info generates a simple note for a rule. Choose this option for mismatches that you want to know about but do not need to correct before final output.
	Inactive never generates an alert message for a rule. Choose this option for mismatches that will not affect the output quality of the PDF document. You must change the state from Inactive to any other state to make the text boxes available.

Preflight Report

After you run a preflight profile, you can create a report describing the potential problems with your document. A report can be a text file, an XML file, or a PDF file. A preflight report provides details on colors, fonts and images used in a document, and lists specific areas likely to cause problems. These errors may cause unexpected results during printing. The preflight report can be used as a guide to make necessary corrections.

Preflight Droplet

A preflight droplet is an application that runs a preflight inspection on one or more PDF files that you drag onto the Droplet icon. When you inspect files using a droplet, you can assign folders to save successful files and problem files. You can also automatically create reports on these files.

The Print Production Toolbar

The Print Production toolbar shown in Figure 5-1includes all the tools that enable a complete PDF workflow for a high color output. The tools on the Print Production toolbar are explained in Table 5-2.

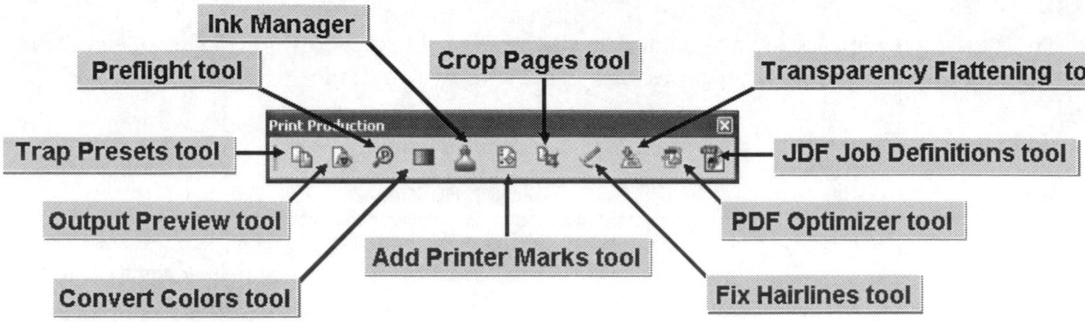

Figure 5-1:

Table 5-2: *Tools on the Print Production toolbar*

Tool	Description
Trap Presets	Enables you to create and apply trap settings to be executed by an Adobe PostScript 3 RIP that licenses Adobe In-RIP Trapping.
Output Preview	Provides controls that are used to preview separations, proof colors, view colors by source, and highlight warning areas for out-of-gamut areas, ink coverage limits, and overprinting all in a dialog box.
Preflight	Allows you to perform more than 400 predefined checks for all the common output errors in a designer's file. Preflight also includes checking for PDF/X compliance, password protection of preflight profiles, PostScript level compatibility, and many other options.
Convert Colors	Converts RGB, CMYK, and Grayscale color spaces to the target color space. You can also choose to embed Adobe PDF documents with ICC profiles.
Ink Manager	The Ink Manager modifies the way inks are treated while the PDF document is open.
Add Printer Marks	Adds standard printer marks to a PDF page for positioning. These marks are applied as content in Acrobat 7.
Crop Pages	Allows you to define the crop, trim, bleed, art, and media boxes on a page. This is important for proper page positioning and placement of printer marks.
Fix Hairlines	Finds hairlines and replaces them with heavier weight lines.

Tool	Description
Transparency Flattening	Provides flattener settings to control the amount of rasterization that occurs during print output or exporting to certain file formats, such as EPS. This tool also includes a preview that lets the users view and control how transparent objects will appear on print.
PDF Optimizer	Provides many settings for inspecting, analyzing, and repairing documents, and reducing the size of PDF files.
JDF Job Definitions	Allows you to create custom job definitions that can be edited and used in a production environment.

The Fix Hairlines Tool

Hairlines are very thin lines in PDF documents that may not appear in the printed output. The Fix Hairlines tool can find hairlines in a document and replace them with a thicker line. You can also use this tool to replace hairlines in Type3 fonts and PostScript patterns. However, font characters and patterns can be used in different contexts in the same document, so changing the line width may produce unexpected results.

How to Preflight Documents

Procedure Reference: Run an Existing Preflight Profile

To run an existing preflight profile:

1. With a document open, display the Preflight dialog box, using one of the following methods:
   - Choose Tools→Print Production→Preflight;
   - Or, in the Print Production toolbar, click the Preflight button;
   - Or, choose Advanced→Preflight.
2. In the Select A Profile For Preflighting The Current PDF list box, select a profile.
3. Execute the profile using one of the following methods:
   - Click the Execute button;
   - Or, click Options and choose Execute Preflight Profile;
   - Or, double-click the selected profile.

Procedure Reference: Unlock a Rule

To unlock a rule:

1. With a document open, display the Preflight dialog box.
2. In the Preflight dialog box, click Options and choose Edit Preflight Profiles (Advanced).
3. In the Preflight: Edit Profiles dialog box, in the Rules list box, select a profile.
4. Display the Preflight: Edit Rule dialog box:
   - Double-click the rule;
   - Or, click the Edit Rule button.

5. Click Usage to view the profiles that use that rule.
6. Click OK.
7. Click Cancel.
8. To unlock the rule, unlock all profiles to which the rule is assigned.

Procedure Reference: Unlock a Condition

To unlock a condition:

1. With a document open, display the Preflight dialog box.
2. In the Preflight dialog box, click Options and choose Edit Preflight Profiles (Advanced).
3. In the Preflight: Edit Profiles dialog box, in the Rules list box, select a profile.
4. Display the Preflight: Edit Condition dialog box:
   - Double-click the rule;
   - Or, click the Edit Condition button.
5. Click Usage to view the rules and profiles that use the condition.
6. Click OK.
7. Click Cancel.
8. To unlock the condition, unlock all profiles to which the condition is assigned.

Procedure Reference: Create a Custom Preflight Profile

To create a custom preflight profile:

1. With a document open, display the Preflight dialog box.
2. In the Preflight dialog box, click Options and choose Edit Preflight Profiles (Advanced).
3. Create a new profile:
   - Click the Create A New Preflight Profile button;
   - Or, in the Profiles list box, select a profile and click the Duplicate The Selected Profile, to create a new profile with the same initial rules as the selected one.
4. In the Preflight: New Profile or Preflight: Duplicate Profile dialog box, specify a name and description for the profile.
5. If necessary, specify other properties.
6. Click OK.
7. In the Preflight: Edit Profiles dialog box, in the Rules list box, select a rule with the appropriate conditions and click the Assign Rule To Profile button to add a rule to the profile.
8. Repeat step 7 to add as many rules to the profile as desired.
9. If necessary, in the Profiles list box, select a rule assigned to the profile and click the Unassign Rule button to remove the rule. Some rules cannot be deleted from duplicate profiles if they are required for that profile.

To remove a rule assigned to a profile, the rule must first be unlocked.

10. Click Save.
11. Click OK to close the Preflight: Edit Profiles dialog box.

Procedure Reference: Edit a Custom Preflight Profile

To edit a preflight profile:

1. Display the Preflight dialog box.
2. In the Preflight dialog box, click Options and choose Edit Preflight Profiles (Advanced).
3. In the Preflight: Edit Profiles dialog box, in the Profiles list box, select a profile.
4. Display the Preflight: Edit Profile dialog box:
   - Double-click the profile;
   - Or, click the Edit Profile button.
5. If necessary, specify a different name and description for the profile.
6. Click OK.
7. In the Preflight: Edit Profiles dialog box, in the Profiles list box, expand the selected profile to view the rules assigned to a profile.
8. In the Rules list box, select a rule and click the Assign Rule To Profile button to add a rule to the profile.
9. Repeat step 7 to add as many rules to the profile as needed.
10. If necessary, in the Profiles list box, select a rule assigned to the profile and click the Unassign Rule button to remove the rule. Some rules cannot be deleted from duplicate profiles if they are required for that profile.

    To remove a rule assigned to a profile, the rule must first be unlocked.

11. Click Save.
12. Click OK to close the Preflight: Edit Profiles dialog box.

Procedure Reference: Interpret a Preflight Result

To interpret preflight results:

1. Run a preflight profile.
2. In the results list box, mismatches are displayed in the order of Errors, Warnings, Info, and Inactive. Check Show Detailed Information About Document to view detailed information about the document.
3. In the Preflight dialog box, check Show Selected Page Element In Snap View, to view the selected item in the Preflight: Snap View dialog box.
4. If necessary, in the Preflight: Snap View dialog box, from the Background Color drop-down list, select a color to display behind objects.

Procedure Reference: Create a Preflight Report

To create a preflight report:

1. Display the Save As dialog box:
   - In the Preflight dialog box, click Report;
   - Or, click Options and choose Create Report.
2. Specify a name and location for the report.
3. From the Save As Type drop-down list, select the appropriate report type:
   - PDF Report: Creates either a detailed report or a list of problems for each problem object, depending on the options selected. You can also choose to highlight the problems by transparent masks and insert preflight results as comments.
   - XML Report: Creates a structured report. This report can be used in workflow systems that can interpret and process Preflight results.
   - Text Report: Creates a report in ASCII characters that can be opened in a text editor. Each line in the report is indented according to the hierarchy in the Preflight results.
4. Click Save.

Procedure Reference: Create a Preflight Droplet

To create a preflight droplet:

1. Display the Preflight dialog box.
2. In the Preflight dialog box, click Options and choose Create Preflight Droplet.
3. From the Preflight profile drop-down list, select a profile.
4. In the On Success section, specify the appropriate options for when the preflight inspection is successful.
   a. Check the first check box, and from the drop-down list, select an option based on what you want Preflight to do with files that pass the inspection.
   b. Check Create Report And Save In Success Folder and specify the type of report and the details to be included.
   c. Click Success Folder and specify the location where the files that pass the inspection are to be saved.
5. In the On Error section, specify the appropriate options for when the preflight inspection fails.
   a. Check the first check box, and from the drop-down list, select an option based on what you want Preflight to do with files that fail the inspection.
   b. Check Create Report And Save In Error Folder and specify the type of report and the details to be included.
   c. Click Error Folder and specify the location where the files that fail the inspection are to be saved.
6. Click Save.
7. Specify a name and location for the preflight droplet and click Save.

8. To run preflight inspection on a PDF file, drag and drop the PDF file on the Droplet icon that is created at the specified location.

Procedure Reference: Fix Hairlines

To fix hairlines:

1. Display the Fix Hairlines dialog box:
   - Choose Tools→Print Production→Fix Hairlines;
   - Or, on the Print Production toolbar, click the Fix Hairlines button.
2. In the Narrower Than Or Equal To text box, type a value for the hairline width.
3. In the Replace With text box, type the replacement width.
4. From the Units drop-down list, select the unit of measurement.
5. Check Include Type3 Fonts to replace hairlines in Type 3 characters with the same replacement width as other hairlines.
6. Check Include Patterns to replace hairlines in Type 3 patterns with the same replacement width as other hairlines.
7. In the Page Range section, specify the pages to check.
8. Click OK.
9. Click Yes.

ACTIVITY 5-1

Preflighting a Catalog PDF

Activity Time:

10 minutes

Data Files:

- Catalog 2004 Print.pdf

Scenario:

Some designers at Super Fast Wheels have sent documents that have had problems such as low resolution images and extra color plates to your print vendor, which cost time and money in rework. To prevent these types of problems in the future, you've decided to insist on preflighting documents prior to submission to the printing company. To begin preflighting, you discuss the guidelines for file submission with the print vendor. They tell you that they cannot accept PDF files earlier than version 1.3. They also cannot work on files that include transparency, transfer curve, and interactive form fields. Additionally, they cannot work on files that use more than four color plates when separations are created and they prefer images to be at least 250 ppi.

What You Do	How You Do It
1. **Duplicate the List Image Below 250 ppi profile and create a new profile with an appropriate description.**	a. **Choose File→Open.**
	b. **Navigate to the C:\084173Data\Finalizing PDF Files\Activity1\Start folder.**
	c. **Select the Catalog 2004 Print.pdf file and click Open.**
	d. **Choose Advanced→Preflight.**
	e. In the Preflight dialog box, **click Options and choose Edit Preflight Profiles (Advanced).**
	f. In the Preflight: Edit Profiles dialog box, in the Profiles list box, **scroll down and select List Images Below 250 ppi.**
	g. **Click the Duplicate Profile button.**
	h. **Type *List SF Wheels Potential Problems***
	i. **Press Tab and type *Profile for Super Fast Wheels marketing materials.***
	j. **Click OK.**

2. **Apply the print vendor's criteria to the profile and run it on the catalog file.**

   a. In the Profiles list box, **expand List SF Wheels Potential Problems.**

   b. In the Rules list box, **scroll down and select Document Generates More Than Four.**

   c. **Click the Assign Rule To Profile button.**

   d. **Scroll down and select Interactive Form Fields Not Allowed.**

   e. **Click the Assign Rule To Profile button.**

   f. **Scroll down and select PDF Version Number < 1.3.**

   g. **Click the Assign Rule To Profile button.**

   h. **Scroll down and select Uses Transfer Curve.**

   i. **Click the Assign Rule To Profile button.**

   j. **Select Uses Transparency.**

   k. **Click the Assign Rule To Profile button.**

   l. **Click Save.**

   m. **Click OK.**

   n. In the Preflight dialog box, **click Execute** to analyze the document using this profile.

   o. This profile lists problems with image resolution, transparency, and that the document generates more than four printing plates. **Close the Preflight dialog box.**

   p. **Close the file.**

TOPIC B

Create PDF/X-Compliant Files

In the previous topic, you have learned various ways to find the potential problems in your documents that you intend to have commercially printed. Another way to ensure a trouble-free document for prepress is to certify that the document is PDF/X compliant. In this topic, you will create a PDF/X-compliant document.

The steps you have taken so far to generate and inspect PDF documents can help you solve many potential problems in documents that you intend to have commercially printed. Certifying that your document meets the PDF/X standard is a fail-safe way of making sure your document is printable before you hand it off to a print vendor who guarantees PDF/X compatibility.

PDF/X

Definition:

PDF/X is a family of standards for the exchange of PDF files intended for prepress that ensures a PDF/X-compliant document will print without problems. As a subset of the PDF format, it eliminates the most common errors in file preparation, such as fonts not embedded, wrong color space, images missing, overprint or trap issues. Thus, when you hand off a certified PDF/X publication to the print vendor, you can be sure that it will print as intended and will save time and money. PDF/X-1a and PDF/X-3 are the commonly used PDF/X specifications.

Example:

PDF file with only CMYK colors and no color management is PDF/X-1a complaint

PDF file with RGB colors and color management is PDF/X-3 complaint

PDF/X Specifications

PDF/X-1a and PDF/X-3 are the commonly used PDF/X specifications.

Files that are PDF/X-1a compliant have the following characteristics:

- Only CMYK and spot colors (no RGB or CIE L*a*b colors allowed).

- Colors must be targeted to a specific output device (for example, the SWOP coated standard for printing on a web offset press).
- Color management is disallowed.
- All fonts must be embedded in the file.
- Trapping, output intents, and the TrimBox or ArtBox must be specified.
- Transfer functions and halftone screen frequency specifications are disallowed.

Files that are PDF/X-3 compliant have the following characteristics:

- Color management and device-independent color spaces (such as RGB color spaces specified by ICC profiles, CIE L*a*b colors, CalRGB and CalGray) are allowed along with CMYK and spot colors.
- The PDF version must be 1.3 or later.
- All fonts must be embedded in the file.
- Trapping, output intents, and the TrimBox or ArtBox must be specified.
- Transfer functions are disallowed.
- Halftone screen frequency specifications are restricted to certain values.

How to Create PDF/X-Compliant Files

Procedure Reference: Save a PDF File as a PDF/X Compliant File Through Preflighting

To save a PDF file as a PDF/X compliant file through preflighting:

1. With a document open, display the Preflight dialog box.
2. Open the Preflight: Convert to PDF/X dialog box:
   - Click the Convert Current PDF To PDF/X button;
   - Or, click Options and choose Convert Current PDF To PDF/X.
3. Select either to convert the PDF to PDF/X-1a or PDF/X-3.
4. From the Set Output Condition To drop-down list, select the appropriate option.
5. Set the Trapped Key option to either True or False based on whether the file contains trapping information or not.
6. Click OK.
7. If the Save As PDF/X-3 dialog is displayed, navigate to the required location, and click Save.
8. If the Preflight message box is displayed, click OK to view the error result that is generated.

Procedure Reference: Create a PDF/X Compliant File From a Design Application Document

To create a PDF/X compliant file from a design application document:

1. With a document open in a design application, use a prepress-friendly method to generate a PDF document.
2. From the settings drop-down list, choose either PDF/X-1a or PDF/X-3, depending on which you want to create.

3. Continue to perform the steps necessary to create a PDF document. The file you create will be PDF/X compliant.

ACTIVITY 5-2

Creating a PDF/X Compliant File

Activity Time:

10 minutes

Data Files:

- Magazine Ad PS.pdf
- Magazine Ad PS.psd

Scenario:

When you send advertisements to be printed in magazines, it's likely that the printing company have problems with some of the document elements, such as RGB images and transparency, which would have been acceptable to your inhouse print vendor. To ensure that any advertisement you send out for inclusion in a magazine will print without problems, you decide to make them comply to the PDF/X-1a documents.

Since you've already created a PDF file intended for prepress of the Magazine Ad document, you want to use it, if possible. If that doesn't work, you'll need to go back to the original file and generate the PDF/X-1a document using the Adobe PDF printer.

What You Do	How You Do It
1. **Try to create a PDF/X compliant file of the PDF.**	a. **Choose File→Open.**
	b. **Navigate to the C:\084173Data\Finalizing PDF Files\Activity2\Start folder.**
	c. **Select the Magazine Ad PS.pdf file and click Open.**
	d. **Choose Advanced→Preflight.**
	e. **Click the Convert Current PDF To PDF/X button.**
	f. In the Preflight: Convert to PDF/X dialog box, **click OK** to accept the default settings.
	g. The conversion to PDF/X failed because the file uses color other than 4c or spot. In the Preflight message box, **click OK.**
	h. **Close the Preflight dialog box.**

2. **Generate a PDF/X compliant file of the Photoshop file.**	a. **Choose Start→All Programs→Adobe Photoshop 7.0.1.** b. **Choose File→Open.** c. **Navigate to the C:\084173Data\Finalizing PDF Files\Activity2\Start folder.** d. **Select the Magazine Ad PS.psd file and click Open.** e. **Choose File→Print.** f. In the Adobe Photoshop message box, **click Proceed.** g. In the Print dialog box, from the Name drop-down list, **select Adobe PDF.** h. **Click Properties.** i. From the Default Settings drop-down list, **select PDF/X-1a:2001.** j. **Click OK.** k. **Click OK.** l. **Double-click in the File Name text box and type** ***Magazine Ad PDFX1a.pdf*** m. **Navigate to the C:\084173Data\Finalizing PDF Files\Activity2\Solution folder and click Save.**
3. **Verify that the PDF file passes compliance testing.**	a. **Choose Advanced→Preflight.**

b. In the Preflight dialog box, **click the Verify Whether the Current PDF Is PDF/X Compliant button.**

c. In the Preflight dialog box, on the Completely Remove PDF/X Information button, the check mark indicates that the file is PDF/X-Compliant.

d. **Close the Preflight dialog box.**

e. **Close the Magazine Ad PDFX1a.pdf file.**

f. **Close the Magazine Ad PS.pdf file.**

g. **Minimize the Adobe Acrobat Professional window.**

h. In the Adobe Photoshop window, **choose File→Exit.**

i. **Restore the Adobe Acrobat Professional window.**

TOPIC C

Create a Composite

Creative professionals often create a composite PDF prior to sending the file to a commercial printer. In this topic, you will create a composite.

When you can create composite prints from Acrobat, you have the option of printing from the same file you distribute to others. This can provide you with a proof of a document that you will get commercially printed, or the final output for smaller print jobs.

Printer Marks

Definition:

Printer marks are special marks that are used to align separations in film or on press and measure color and ink density. You can add printer marks at print time or embed printer marks in the file. These marks are not actually added to the Adobe PDF file but are included in the output.

Example:

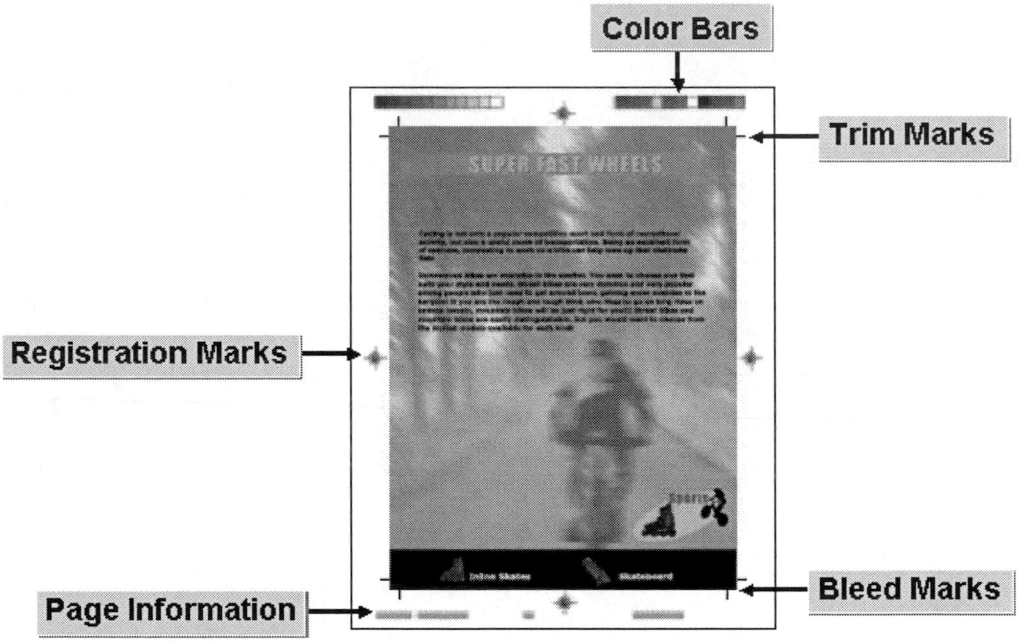

Types of Printer Marks

You can add a variety of printer marks to a PDF document. See Table 5-3.

Table 5-3: *Types of Printer Marks*

Printer Mark	Description
Trim Marks	Trim Marks are fine (hairline) horizontal and vertical rules that define where the page should be trimmed. Trim marks can also help register (align) one color separation to another.
Bleed Marks	Bleed Marks appear a bit outside the trim marks, designating how much bleed is necessary to ensure that color will print till the page edge after trimming.
Registration Marks	Registration Marks are small targets outside the page area for aligning the different separations in a color document.
Color Bars	Color Bars are small squares of color representing the CMYK inks and tints of gray (in 10% increments). Your service provider uses these marks to adjust ink density on the printing press.
Page Information	Page Information labels the film with the name of the file, the time and date of printout, the line screen used, the screen angle for the separation, and the color of each particular plate. These labels appear at the top of the images.

Ink Manager

The Ink Manager lets you assign the trapping sequence and neutral density of each ink for printing. It also lets you assign one ink as an alias of another, so wherever one ink was originally specified, the other will be printed. It can also be used to convert spot colors to process colors.

How to Create a Composite

Procedure Reference: Print a Composite

To print a composite:

1. Choose File→Print.
2. From the Printer drop-down list, choose a printer.
3. Click Properties.
4. Select appropriate Page Size and Orientation settings, and click OK.
5. In the Print dialog box, in the Page Handling section, select options common to all applications.

   Selecting None from the Page Scaling drop-down list prevents the page size from being scaled to fit on the paper.

6. Click Advanced.
7. In the Advanced Print Setup dialog box, select Output and choose settings appropriate for composite printing:
   - From the Color drop-down list, select Composite (for PostScript printers) or Composite Gray (for non-PostScript printers).

- From the Color Profile drop-down list, choose Same As Source for no color management, Printer/Postscript Color management to use the printer's built-in color handling, or choose a color profile appropriate to the printer you're using.
- Check the Apply Output Preview Settings check box to simulate the print space defined using the Tools→Print Production→Output Preview command. This enables one printer to emulate another's output (for example, to simulate the press colors on a desktop printer).
- If your printer doesn't natively support overprinting, check the Simulate Overprinting check box to simulate the effects of overprinting.
- If your document contains trapping annotations, check the Emit Trap Annotations check box to send trapping annotations information to a PostScript printing device that supports the in-RIP trapping.
- Check the Use Maximum Available JPEG2000 Image Resolution check box, to generate PostScript using the maximum resolution data contained in the image. If this option is unchecked the resolution data is consistent with the resolution settings specified on the Transparency Flattening panel.
- Specify appropriate Ink Manager settings to modify the way inks are treated.

8. In the Advanced Print Setup dialog box, select Marks And Bleeds and specify the printer's marks and the style to be included.
9. In the Advanced Print Setup dialog box, select Transparency Flattening and specify settings to control how transparent areas are output.
10. In the Advanced Print Setup dialog box, select PostScript Options and choose settings appropriate for composite printing.
11. If desired, save the settings you've chosen by clicking Save As, typing a name in the Save Print Settings As text box, and clicking OK.
12. Click OK to close the Advanced Print Setup dialog box.
13. Click OK.

ACTIVITY 5-3

Printing a Composite

Activity Time:

10 minutes

Data Files:

- Catalog 2004 Print.pdf

Scenario:

Before sending documents out for commercial printing, you'd like to check them by printing a composite proof on your desktop printer, a Tektronix Phaser 480X. Since you want to check the document's bleed and trim, you include printer's marks on the output. To ensure that the page will fit on the paper at full size including the printer's marks, you'll need to print to tabloid size paper instead of letter size paper in most instances. Additionally, you want to print the output to another PDF file instead of the printer in instances where the document doesn't need close scrutiny and you want to save money or time, such as for the Catalog 2004 Print.pdf file.

What You Do	How You Do It
1. **Set up the catalog file to print to your desktop printer.**	a. **Choose File→Open.**
	b. **Navigate to the C:\084173Data\Finalizing PDF Files\Activity3\Start folder.**
	c. **Select the Catalog 2004 Print.pdf file and click Open.**
	d. **Choose File→Print.**
	e. From the Name drop-down list, **select Tektronix Phaser 480X.**
	f. **Click Properties.**
	g. **Click Advanced.**
	h. From the Paper Size drop-down list, **select Tabloid.**
	i. **Click OK.**
	j. **Select the Layout tab.**

k. In the Orientation section, **verify that Portrait is selected.**

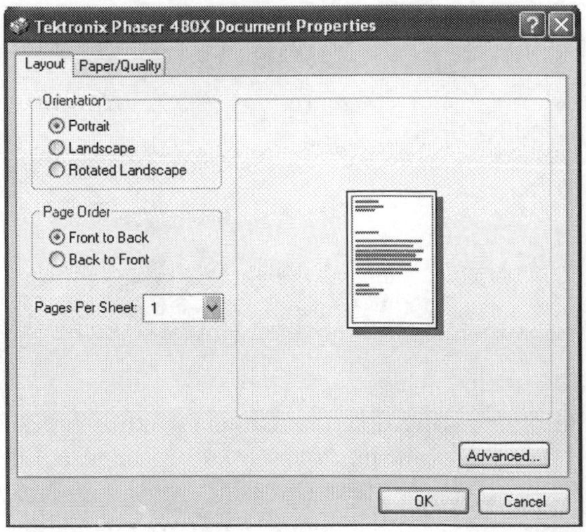

l. **Click OK** to return to the Print dialog box.

m. In the Page Handling section, from the Page Scaling drop-down list, **select None.**

n. **Click Advanced.**

o. **Verify that Composite is selected in the Color drop-down list, 300lpi 300dpi is selected in the Screening drop-down list, and Printer/PostScript Color Management is selected in the Color Profile drop-down list.**

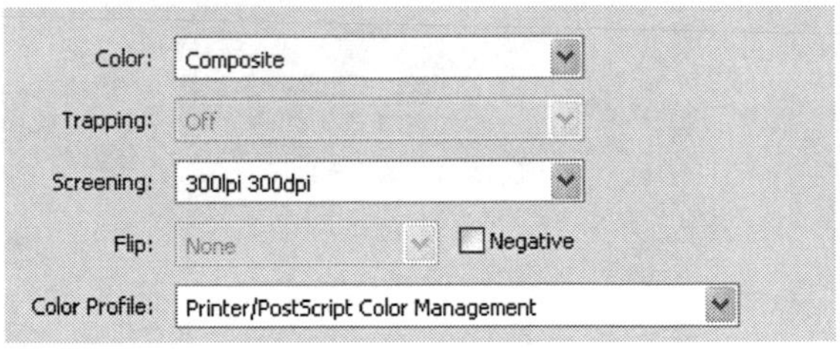

p. In the Advanced Print Setup dialog box, to the left, **select Marks And Bleeds.**

q. **Check All Marks.**

2.	**Save the settings you chose to a custom setting named Composite Proof.**	a. **Click Save As.** b. In the Save Print Settings As text box, **type *Composite Proof* and click OK.** c. **Click OK.**
3.	**Print a new PDF file that simulates the output you'd get if you printed to the Tektronix printer.**	a. From the Name drop-down list, **select Adobe PDF.** b. **Click Properties.** c. From the Default Settings drop-down list, **select Magazine 133 lpi, CM and click OK.** d. **Click OK** to display the Save PDF File As dialog box. e. In the File Name text box, **type *Catalog 2004 Composite Print.pdf*** f. **Navigate to the C:\084173Data\Finalizing PDF Files\Activity3\Solution folder and click Save.** g. **Close the Catalog 2004 Composite Print.pdf file.** h. **Close the Catalog 2004 Print.pdf file.**

TOPIC D

Create Color Separations

Your commercial printer requires that you provide color separations for your document. In this topic, you will create color separations targeted for a specific printer.

While many print providers generate color separations themselves, some only handle the press work, preferring that you or a service bureau do the prepress work and provide separations film. Even if you are not responsible for creating the final separations used for printing, you may want to print them so you can verify their output prior to handing off the document or to send to the print provider as an example.

How to Create Color Separations

Procedure Reference: Create Color Separations

To create color separations:

1. Choose File→Print.
2. From the Name drop-down list, select a printer.
3. Click Properties.
4. Select appropriate Layout and Paper/Quality settings, and click OK.
5. In the Page Handling section, from the Page Scaling drop-down list, select None to avoid having the page size scaled to fit on the paper.
6. Click Advanced to display the Advanced Print Setup dialog box.
7. In the Advanced Print Setup dialog box, select Output and choose settings appropriate for color separations printing:
   - From the Color drop-down list, choose Separations.
   - From the Screening drop-down list, select a combination of halftone screen and printer resolution value.
   - From the Flip drop-down list, select the appropriate image exposure option.
   - Check the Negative check box to print "white on black," which is commonly used for printing color separation film in the United States.
8. In the Ink Manager section, the default selection of Emit All Plates in the Plate Control drop-down list, specifies that all inks are selected at once. To create a separation for a particular ink color, uncheck the check box to the left of all other ink colors.
9. In the Advanced Print Setup dialog box, select Transparency Flattening and specify settings to control how transparent areas are output
10. In the Advanced Print Setup dialog box, select PostScript Options and specify settings appropriate for composite printing.
11. If necessary, click Save As, type a name in the Save Print Settings As text box, and click OK to save the setting.
12. Click OK to close the Advanced Print Setup dialog box.

13. Click OK.
14. Click OK to print the file.

ACTIVITY 5-4

Printing Color Separations

Activity Time:

10 minutes

Data Files:

- Catalog 2004 Print.pdf

Scenario:

In addition to the composite print you created, you'd like to check how color separations of the Catalog 2004 Print.pdf file will appear in print, using an AGFA imagesetter. Since you don't have that imagesetter in house, you'll print a PDF simulation.

Since you'll use most of the same settings as you used for the composite print, including the color management and printer marks settings, you'll modify the Composite Proof setting to create a new Color Separations setting. You'll output the file as a negative, since you're used to looking at color separations as negative film. You'll set the screening as you would use for the real print job, to 133 lpi and 2400 dpi.

What You Do	How You Do It
1. **Set the catalog file to print to an AGFA imagesetter.**	a. **Choose File→Open.**
	b. **Navigate to the C:\084173Data\Finalizing PDF Files\Activity4\Start folder.**
	c. **Select the Catalog 2004 Print.pdf file and click Open.**
	d. **Choose File→Print.**
	e. From the Name drop-down list, **select AGFA AccuSet 1500.**
	f. **Click Properties.**
	g. **Click Advanced.**

h. **Verify that the Paper Size drop-down list is set to Tabloid and click OK.**

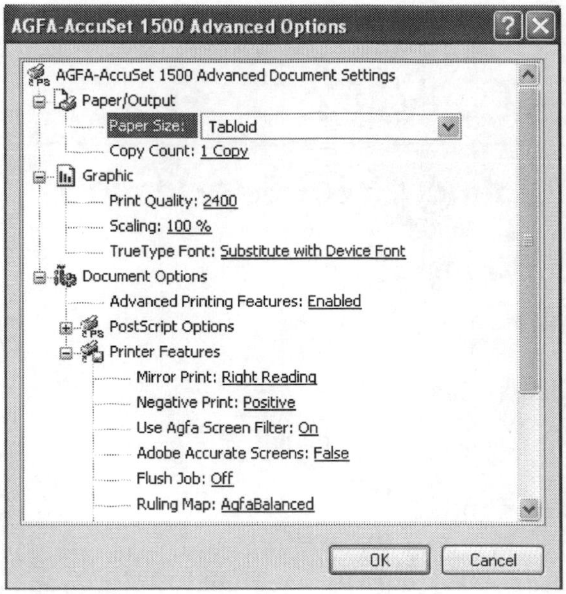

i. **Click OK** to return to the Print dialog box.

j. **Verify that the Page Scaling drop-down list is set to None.**

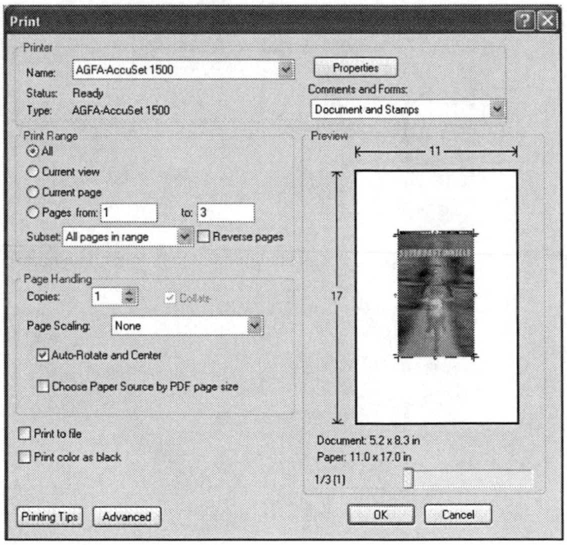

2. **Starting from the Composite Proof setting, create a new Color Separations setting.**

   a. **Click Advanced.**

   b. From the Settings drop-down list, **select Composite Proof.**

   c. In the Advanced Print Setup dialog box, **select Output.**

   d. From the Color drop-down list, **select Separations.**

   e. From the Screening drop-down list, **select 133lpi 2400dpi.**

   f. **Check Negative.**

   g. **Click the Color Profile drop-down arrow.**

   h. **Scroll down and select U.S. Web Coated (SWOP) V2.**

   i. **Click Save As.**

   j. In the Save Print Settings As text box, **type *Color Separations* and click OK.**

   k. **Click OK.**

3. **Print a PDF file that simulates the output you'd get if you printed to the AGFA printer.**
   a. From the Name drop-down list, **select Adobe PDF.**
   b. **Click Properties.**
   c. From the Default Settings drop-down list, **select Press Quality and click OK.**
   d. **Click OK.**
   e. In the File Name text box, **type *Catalog 2004 Separations Print.pdf***
   f. Navigate to the C:\084173Data\Finalizing PDF Files\Activity4\Solution folder and **click Save** to view the PDF that is generated.
   g. **Close the Catalog 2004 Separations Print.pdf file.**
   h. **Close the Catalog 2004 Print.pdf file.**

Lesson 5 Follow-up

In this lesson, you preflighted a PDF document, established compliance with the PDF/X standard, and printed both composites and color separations. These skills will enable you to create finished documents, proofs, and color plates for printing on a press.

1. **Do you expect to print composites or color separations more frequently? Why?**

2. **Which settings in the Advanced Print Setup dialog box should be correct to get your desired printed output? Why?**

Follow-up

In this course, you created PDF files for a variety of purposes, including for online distribution, for receiving user feedback via forms, and for prepress. Lastly, you learned to create both composite prints and color separations from PDF documents. These skills will enable you to generate and distribute files in PDF format that work flawlessly for the purposes you intend them.

1. **Of the tools covered in this course, which one did you like the most? Why?**

2. **What new information about working with Acrobat was the most valuable to you?**

3. **What do you think is the biggest advantage of using Acrobat? Why?**

What's Next?

This is the last course in this series.

NOTES

APPENDIX A

Adobe Certified Expert (ACE) Program®

Adobe® Acrobat® 7.0 ACE Exam Objectives

The Adobe Certified Expert (ACE) Program is for graphic designers, web designers, developers, systems integrators, value-added resellers, and business professionals who seek recognition for their expertise with specific Adobe products. Certification candidates must pass a product proficiency exam in order to become Adobe Certified Experts.

Selected Element K courseware addresses product-specific exam objectives. The following table indicates where Acrobat 7.0 exam objectives are covered in Element K courseware. For example, 1A indicates that the objective is addressed in Lesson 1, Topic A.

Adobe Acrobat Professional 7.0 with Print Production

Exam Topics	Acrobat 7.0: Level 1, 084172	Acrobat 7.0: Level 2, 084173
1.0 Navigating and customizing the Acrobat User Interface		
1.1 Change the appearance of the work area.	1A	
1.2 Change how navigation tabs are displayed.	1A	
1.3 Open and use the How To window.	1C	
1.4 Describe how to search for topics in the Help system.	1C	
1.5 Set application preferences by configuring options for categories in the Preferences dialog box.	1A, 6B	
2.0 Creating PDF documents		

Exam Topics	Acrobat 7.0: Level 1, 084172	Acrobat 7.0: Level 2, 084173
2.1 Given a scenario, configure settings in the Acrobat PDF Maker dialog box to create a PDF document from a Microsoft Office application.	2A	
2.2 Create a PDF document from a Web page.	2C	
2.3 Create a PDF document from a scanner.	2A	
2.4 Create a PDF document from multiple documents.	2D	
2.5 Discuss font embedding and substitution and issues related to fonts within a PDF document.	2A	
3.0 Creating and validating accessible PDF documents		
3.1 Add tags to a PDF document such that it will be accessible.		2E
3.2 Validate an accessible PDF document and correct issues as required.		2E
3.3 Describe the features provided by Acrobat to aid individuals in viewing or printing a PDF document.		2E
4.0 Viewing and navigating PDF documents		
4.1 Given a tool used for viewing or navigating, describe the functionality and how to use the tool to navigate a PDF document.	1A, 1B	
4.2 Add navigation features to a PDF document.	4A-4D	
4.3 Configure viewing and navigation options for PDF documents that will be viewed in a web browser.	6A	
4.4 Use the Organizer to locate a specific PDF document.	5A	
4.5 Navigate through a PDF document by using Search/Find.	1C	
5.0 Modifying and enhancing PDF documents		
5.1 Reduce the size of a PDF document by using the PDF Optimizer.		2C
5.2 Edit text by using the TouchUp Text tool.	3B	

Exam Topics	Acrobat 7.0: Level 1, 084172	Acrobat 7.0: Level 2, 084173
5.3 Explain how to modify PDF documents by selecting options from menus in the Document menu.	3A	
5.4 Attach files to a PDF document.	6B	
5.5 Incorporate headers, footers, watermarks and backgrounds to a PDF document.	3C, 6B	
6.0 Reviewing and commenting		
6.1 Explain how to setup a browser-based review of an Adobe PDF document.	Appendix B Topic B	
6.2 Explain how to setup an E-mail-based review of an Adobe PDF document.	Appendix B Topic A	
6.3 Add comments to an Adobe PDF document.	6D	
7.0 Managing document security		
7.1 List and describe methods that can be used to secure a PDF document by using passwords.	6C	
7.2 List and describe methods that can be used to secure a PDF document by using PKI and certificates.	6C	
7.3 Explain how Policy Server is used to encrypt PDF documents and manage Digital Rights Management.	6C	
7.4 Manage security by using security policies.	6C	
8.0 Working with digital signatures		
8.1 Create a signature field on a PDF document.	6C	
8.2 Apply a signature to a PDF document.	6C	
8.3 Use document certificates to certify a document.	6C	
9.0 Using Distiller to create PDF documents		
9.1 Given a specific output requirement, choose the correct Distiller job option.		4D
9.2 Given a setting in the File Options section of the General panel, explain when you would use that setting.		4D

Exam Topics	Acrobat 7.0: Level 1, 084172	Acrobat 7.0: Level 2, 084173
9.3 Given a scenario, manage how images are handled by selecting the appropriate settings in the Images panel.		4D
9.4 Given a specific output requirement, create a customized job option.		4D
10.0 Using Adobe PDF printer to create PDF documents		
10.1 Explain the relationship between the Adobe PDF printer and Distiller.		4D
10.2 Explain how print driver settings impact the behavior of Distiller.		4D
11.0 Using Adobe PDF Maker to create PDF documents		
11.1 Given a scenario, create a PDF document by customizing settings in PDF Maker.	2A	
11.2 Create a PDF document ready for high quality print production/separation from PDF Maker supported applications.	2A	
12.0 Managing Color		
12.1 Explain the purpose of the Simulation Profile setting in the Output Preview dialog box, and how you should determine which profile to select.		4E
12.2 Explain the purpose of the Simulate Ink Black and Simulate Paper White options in the Output Preview dialog box.		4E
12.3 Given a scenario, manage color in a PDF document by selecting the appropriate settings in the Color panel.		4D
13.0 Managing transparency		
13.1 Explain the difference between Distiller created PDF and native PDF with respect to live and flattened transparency.		4A
13.2 Given a scenario, select the appropriate settings in the Flattener Preview dialog box and apply transparency flattening.		4A
14.0 Using Output Preview		

Exam Topics	Acrobat 7.0: Level 1, 084172	Acrobat 7.0: Level 2, 084173
14.1 Discuss the features of, and explain when and how to respond to an overprint warning.		4E
14.2 Discuss the features of, and explain when and how to respond to a rich black warning.		4E
14.3 Explain how to use Separations Preview.		4E
14.4 Given a scenario, troubleshoot a PDF document that has too many colors or has unexpected results with respect to separations.		5A
15.0 Preflighting PDF documents		
15.1 Given a scenario, create a preflight profile.		5A
15.2 Explain how to create and use a preflight report to detect problems in a PDF document.		5A
15.3 Give examples of what would cause a file to fail during validation.		5A
15.4 Describe the functionality and create a preflight droplet.		5A
15.5 Given a scenario determine if you should use a default profile or create a custom profile.		5A
15.6 Describe the industry standards used for preflight profiles.		5A
16.0 Correcting PDF documents for print output		
16.1 Specify the correct settings and add printer marks to a PDF document.		5C
16.2 Modify how inks are handled in a PDF document by using the Ink Manager.		5D
16.3 Discuss issues related to and fix hairlines by using the Fix Hairlines tool.		5A

Adobe Acrobat Professional 7.0 with Adobe Designer

Exam Topics	Acrobat 7.0: Level 1, 084172	Acrobat 7.0: Level 2, 084173
1.0 Navigating and customizing the Acrobat User Interface		

Appendix A

Exam Topics	Acrobat 7.0: Level 1, 084172	Acrobat 7.0: Level 2, 084173
1.1 Change the appearance of the work area.	1A	
1.2 Change how navigation tabs are displayed.	1A	
1.3 Open and use the How To window.	1C	
1.4 Describe how to search for topics in the Help system.	1C	
1.5 Set application preferences by configuring options for categories in the Preferences dialog box.	1A, 6B	
2.0 Creating PDF documents		
2.1 Given a scenario, configure settings in the Acrobat PDF Maker dialog box to create a PDF document from a Microsoft Office application.	2A	
2.2 Create a PDF document from a web page.	2C	
2.3 Create a PDF document from a scanner.	2A	
2.4 Create a PDF document from multiple documents.	2D	
2.5 Discuss font embedding and substitution and issues related to fonts within a PDF document.	2A	
3.0 Creating and validating accessible PDF documents		
3.1 Add tags to a PDF document such that it will be accessible.		2E
3.2 Validate an accessible PDF document and correct issues as required.		2E
3.3 Describe the features provided by Acrobat to aid individuals in viewing or printing a PDF document.		2E
4.0 Viewing and navigating PDF documents		
4.1 Given a tool used for viewing or navigating, describe the functionality and how to use the tool to navigate a PDF document.	1A, 1B	
4.2 Add navigation features to a PDF document.	4A-4D	

Exam Topics	Acrobat 7.0: Level 1, 084172	Acrobat 7.0: Level 2, 084173
4.3 Configure viewing and navigation options for PDF documents that will be viewed in a Web browser.	2C	
4.4 Use the Organizer to locate a specific PDF document.	5A	
4.5 Navigate through a PDF document by using Search/Find.	1C	
5.0 Modifying and enhancing PDF documents		
5.1 Reduce the size of a PDF document by using the PDF Optimizer.		2C
5.2 Edit text by using the TouchUp Text tool.	3B	
5.3 Explain how to modify PDF documents by selecting options from menus in the Document menu.	3A	
5.4 Attach files to a PDF document.	6B	
5.5 Incorporate headers, footers, watermarks and backgrounds to a PDF document.	3C, 6B	
6.0 Reviewing and commenting		
6.1 Explain how to setup a browser-based review of an Adobe PDF document.	Appendix B Topic B	
6.2 Explain how to setup an E-mail based review of an Adobe PDF document.	Appendix B Topic A	
6.3 Add comments to an Adobe PDF document.	6D	
7.0 Managing document security		
7.1 List and describe methods that can be used to secure a PDF document by using passwords.	6C	
7.2 List and describe methods that can be used to secure a PDF document by using PKI and certificates.	6C	
7.3 Explain how Policy Server is used to encrypt PDF documents and manage Digital Rights Management.	6C	
7.4 Manage security by using security policies.	6C	
8.0 Working with digital signatures		

Exam Topics	Acrobat 7.0: Level 1, 084172	Acrobat 7.0: Level 2, 084173
8.1 Create a signature field on a PDF document.	6C	
8.2 Apply a signature to a PDF document.	6C	
8.3 Use document certificates to certify a document.	6C	
9.0 Advanced printing tools		
9.1 List and describe the steps required to produce color separations.		5D
9.2 List and describe the features and options made available through the Print Production toolbar.		5A
9.3 Explain how to incorporate a color management workflow into the process of creating PDF Documents.		4C
10.0 Validating PDF content		
10.1 List and describe the options provided by the Adobe Preflight feature.		5A
10.2 Describe the steps necessary to validate PDF content for output to a press or other output device		5A
10.3 List and describe the options Adobe Acrobat provides for creating PDF/X-compliant files.		5B
11.0 Customizing the Form Designer environment		
11.1 Move, dock and resize palettes.		3A
11.2 Given a scenario, customize toolbars.		3A
11.3 Modify how objects are aligned by setting up grids and measurement units.		3D
11.4 Change the display of guidelines and object boundaries.		3D
12.0 Creating forms		
12.1 Compare and contrast the features Adobe Designer provides for creating forms versus Acrobat forms.		3A

Exam Topics	Acrobat 7.0: Level 1, 084172	Acrobat 7.0: Level 2, 084173
12.2 Explain when you would use Adobe Designer to create a form versus when you would use Acrobat to create a form.		3A
12.3 Given a scenario, setup Master and Body pages.		3A
12.4 Explain how to place an object from the Library palette on a form.		3A
12.5 Add an image to a form.		3A
12.6 Add text to a form.		3B
12.7 Select and move objects that are on a form.		3A, 3B
12.8 Given a scenario, change the properties of an object on a form.		3A
13.0 Editing forms		
13.1 Align objects with other objects or to a grid.		3B
13.2 Group and ungroup objects, and add objects to an existing group.		3B, 3D
13.3 Resize objects including making objects the same size.		3C
13.4 Select and change the properties of multiple objects.		3B
13.5 Delete an object.		3B
13.6 Copy objects.		3B
13.7 Lock objects.		3B
14.0 Previewing, testing, and using forms		
14.1 Describe the differences between how users with Adobe Reader can use forms versus users with Adobe Acrobat.		3A
14.2 Given a scenario, set the properties for a form by selecting the appropriate options in the Forms Properties dialog box.		3A
14.3 List and describe the different formats in which forms can be saved, and when you would select a particular format.		3A

NOTES

LESSON LABS

Due to classroom setup constraints, some labs cannot be keyed in sequence immediately following their associated lesson. Your instructor will tell you whether your labs can be practiced immediately following the lesson or whether they require separate setup from the main lesson content.

LESSON 1 LAB 1

Creating a PDF of the Sprinkler System White Paper

Objective:

Data Files:

- ElecPlan.pdf
- Sprinkler Subsystem.vsd
- Sprinkler Decision Tree.vsd

Scenario:

You are a supervisor at Pellick Design Group, and one of your group members has given you a PDF document created from an AutoCAD drawing of an electrical system. You need to quickly check the drawing's details before you can approve it. Among other things, you want to check that the area of the client's tenant space, surrounded by a cloud notation Figure 1-A is approximately 3000 square feet as intended.

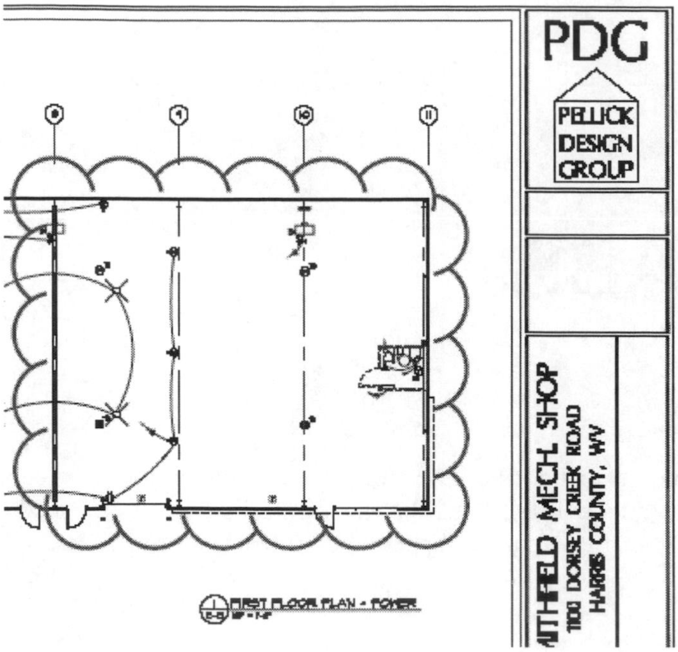

Figure 1-A: *You want to measure the approximate area of this tenant space.*

Also, you have received two files pertaining to research and development work on sprinkler system design created in Visio. Before you approve it, you wish to convert these files into PDF and view the layers.

1. **Use Acrobat to open the ElecPlan.pdf file, located within the C:\084173Data\Technical Documents\Lab1\Start folder.**

2. **Hide the Electrical layer set to make it easier to view the overall design without distraction.**

3. **View the scale of the drawing (located just to the left of the word "Smithfield" in the title block on the right) with the main document zoomed so you can view the entire drawing.**

4. **Determine the approximate area in square feet of the space shown in the cloud notation Figure 1-A.**

5. **Close the file.**

6. **Convert the Sprinkler Subsystem.vsd and Sprinkler Decision Tree.vsd Visio documents to PDF, retaining layers.**

7. **Use the Layers pane to examine the PDF document.**

LESSON 2 LAB 1

Enhancing PDF Documents for Various Clients

Objective:

Data Files:

- kitchenkreativscatalog.pdf
- applemachine.mov
- Zing Ad.pdf
- NAU Brochure.pdf

Scenario:

You have designed PDF documents for various clients, including Zing, North Atlantic University, and KitchenKreativs. You'll now enhance the PDF files for those companies for online use.

1. **Add the applemachine.mov move to the Slice It page in the kitchenkreativscatalog.pdf document.**
2. **Create an action to make the applemachine.mov movie play automatically when the Slice It page appears.**
3. **Optimize the PDF file.**
4. **Move the Zing Ad.pdf and NAU Brochure.pdf documents to the Enhancing PDF\Lab2\Start folder, and apply a batch process to add a watermark to each one to identify them as preliminary drafts.**
5. **Add tags to the NAU Brochure.pdf document and check the document for accessibility.**
6. **Reflow the NAU Brochure.pdf document and ensure that the order of each page's text and graphics makes basic sense, and fix any significant problems with the reflow order.**

Lesson 3 Lab 1

Creating a Membership Form

Objective:

Data Files:

- KitchenKreativsLogo

Scenario:

KitchenKreativs has asked you to create a form to collect personal details from people browsing their website. You are planning to create this interactive form in Adobe Designer.

1. **Create a new form in Adobe Designer using all the default settings.**
2. **Click and drag the Submit By Email button to the bottom of the page and add the KitchenKreativsLogo.Gif file to the top of the page.**
3. **Create text fields below the image object and to the left of the Layout Editor. The text fields must be arranged one below the other with appropriate settings and should have the caption Name, Address, Email, and Phone No.**
4. Create a drop-down list object below the text field objects. This drop-down list needs to have the countries Canada, Mexico, Germany, Australia, and Brazil listed in it. Set Canada as the default value.
5. **Specify the country code for each of the countries as their On values. The country codes are listed below:**
   - Canada: 1
   - Mexico: 52
   - Germany: 49
   - Australia: 61
   - Brazil: 55
6. **Create a text field to the right of the drop-down list and label it as Country Code. Create a script in the drop-down list that would display the value of the selected country in the Country Code text box as soon as the selection is made.**
7. **Create a radio button group below the drop-down list that would allow users to choose their Gender.**
8. **Group all objects together.**
9. **Create a Reset Button to the right of the Submit By Email button.**

10. Save the file as KitchenKreativs.pdf.

11. Open the form in Acrobat, key in the sample data on it, save it, and view the collected data in a spreadsheet.

LESSON 4 LAB 1

Preparing Documents for Commercial Printing

Data Files:

- Zing Ad PS.psd
- NAU Brochure.pdf
- Zing Photo.jpeg

Scenario:

You need to prepare documents for two of your clients, Zing and North Atlantic University, for commercial printing.

1. Create a set of Adobe PDF settings named Zing Press Settings, which downsamples color and grayscale images above 400 pixels-per-inch down to 275 pixels-per-inch.

2. Use the Zing Press Settings to generate a PDF file from the Zing Ad PS.psd file for prepress.

3. Check that the working RGB color space is set to sRGB IEC61966-2.1 to reflect the color space that those clients have requested you work in.

4. Preview color separations of the NAU Brochure.pdf file on screen.

Lesson 5 Lab 1

Finalizing the Zing Advertisement for Commercial Printing

Data Files:

- Zing Ad PS.pdf

Scenario:

To finalize the Zing advertisement for commercial printing, you also need to print a composite proof of the Zing Ad PS.pdf file to letter size paper on the Tektronix Phaser 480X printer without printer marks. In addition to the composite print, you want to generate color separations of the document as they'll appear printed using an AGFA imagesetter. Since you don't have that imagesetter in house, you'll print a PDF simulation. You'll use most of the same settings as you used for the composite print, but will add printer's marks. You'll output the file as a negative, since you're used to looking at color separations as negative film. You'll set the screening as you'd use for the real print job, to 150 lpi and 3000 dpi.

1. **Run a preflight inspection of the Zing Ad PS.pdf file using a profile that checks for a minimum image resolution of 250 pixels-per-inch and for images that are not saved in the CMYK color mode.**
2. **Generate a PDF/X-compatible file from the Zing Ad PS.pdf file.**
3. **Print a PDF simulation of a composite of the Zing Ad PS.pdf file as it would appear printed to the Tektronix printer.**
4. **Print a PDF simulation of color separations of the Zing Ad PS.pdf file as it would appear printed to the AGFA printer.**

SOLUTIONS

Lesson 1

Activity 1-2

1. **What are the additional components installed in AutoCAD during a default installation of Adobe Acrobat Professional?**

    a) The Adobe PDF menu and the Convert From AutoCAD buttons.

    ✓ b) The Convert To PDF buttons and the Adobe PDF menu.

    c) The Convert To PDF From AutoCAD buttons and the Adobe PDF menu.

    d) The Adobe PDF menu and the Convert PDF buttons.

2. **How can you change the settings specified for converting AutoCAD documents to the PDF format?**

    Choose Adobe PDF→Change Conversion Settings and specify settings for the generated PDF document's attributes.

3. **How can you convert an AutoCAD document to PDF?**

    Click one of the Convert To Adobe PDF buttons on the toolbar; or choose one of the Convert To Adobe PDF commands from the Adobe PDF menu; or type PDF in the AutoCAD command line.

Lesson 2

Activity 2-1

1. **True or False? You could use either Acrobat 6 or Acrobat 5 compatibility to achieve the objectives for the movie clip you are adding.**

    __ True

    ✓ False

Activity 2-6

2. **Which page seems to have most content in an illogical order, and what might you do to address the problem?**

    On page 3, a story about a marriage is in the middle of a story on a recipe for lemonade and its graphics. You could either move the "Cilantro's Couple Marries" story below the recipe, or move the recipe above the "Cilantro's Couple Marries" text.

Lesson 3

Activity 3-1

3. **Based on the default settings in the New Form Assistant, which button is automatically added to the new form?**

   a) HTTP Submit button

   ✓ b) Submit By Email button

   c) Print button

   d) Reset button

Activity 3-4

7. **True or False? When the Specify Item Values check box is unchecked, the On values will match the caption of the radio button.**

   _✓_ True

   __ False

Lesson 4

Activity 4-1

1. **Arrange in sequence the different stages of the commercial printing process.**

   _5_ Print color separations

   _3_ Create trapping and overprinting

   _4_ Create proofs

   _6_ Print document on press

   _1_ Choose workflow options

   _2_ Create document

2. **Which process divides colors into ink components for printing each ink separately?**

   ✓ a) Color separation

   b) Trapping

   c) Composite color printing

   d) Transparency

3. **True or False? Objects in the background are partially or fully visible through transparent objects.**

   _✓_ True

   __ False

Activity 4-2

1. **Which of the following methods are appropriate for creating the PDF file for prepress purposes?**

   ✓ a) Open the Magazine Ad PS.psd document in Photoshop, and print directly to PDF.

   b) In Acrobat, generate a pdf file of the Magazine Ad PS.psd file using the Create PDF drop-down list on the Tasks toolbar.

   ✓ c) Open the Magazine Ad PS.psd document, and generate the PDF file by saving directly to PDF in the Save As dialog box.

   ✓ d) Print a postscript file and distill it manually.

3. **What makes the PDF file generated from the JPEG file composite inappropriate for prepress.**

   ✓ a) It is entirely composed of a raster image

   b) Includes vector art

   ✓ c) Contains gray colored pixels around the characters of the body text

   d) Includes text

GLOSSARY

Accessibility Setup Assistant
A wizard that enables users to change the on-screen appearance of PDFs and how they are handled by a screen reader, screen magnifier, or other assistive technology.

action
A step you set up to occur automatically when the PDF file encounters a specific trigger.

Adobe Designer
A client-based, point-and-click tool you can use for creating graphical forms.

bleed
To print color that extends all the way to the edges of the final printed piece. To create a bleed, the publication is printed on oversized paper with color extending past the intended page edges, then trimmed to size, cutting off a bit of color at the edges.

color management
An option in the Preferences dialog box that is used to make colors match consistently between devices, such as a computer monitor, and a printer's output.

color separation
The process of dividing colors into ink components for the purpose of printing each ink separately.

composite color printing
The process of printing to a device that outputs directly to a page, combining all of the color inks onto the finished medium at once.

condition
A simple statement that is either true or false for a given object in a PDF document.

Flattening
A technology that blends overlapping objects, which have transparency applied to them, into one flat set of opaque objects.

ICC profile
A standard format for a color profile, created by the International Color Consortium, which defines a device's color space.

layer
An object used to display information in a PDF document.

Layout Editor
The area where you create the body and master pages for the form design.

palette
A feature that provides easy access to frequently used tools and includes one or more tabs with property information.

PDF Optimizer
A command that is used to minimize PDF file size by compressing the file and its constituent parts (images, fonts, so on.) so that it can be viewed quickly by the end user.

PDF/X
A family of standards for the exchange of PDF files intended for prepress that ensures a PDF/X-compliant document will print without problems.

preflight profile
A set of criteria that defines acceptable values for a document.

printer marks
Special marks that are used to align separations in film or on press and measure color and ink density.

Reflow
The order in which the elements of a PDF document are displayed on smaller displays without having to scroll horizontally to read each line.

structured document
A document that contains a logical structure tree, which defines the intended reading order and hierarchy of information within.

tagged PDF document
A document organized into a logical tree structure containing articles, figures, sections, and subsections.

transparency
Any editable area within a document that is less than completely opaque.

trapping
The process of ensuring that adjoining color areas overlap slightly to prevent white gaps from appearing between colors.

INDEX

Q

R

S

T

V

W

NOTES